Parenting:
If it's Hard,
You're Doing it Right!

Raising Kids with Communication, Empathy and Accountability

D1707440

(blank)

For Amélie and Olivia

My two reasons for everything I do

Table of Contents

When I was 5 years old, my mother told me that happiness was the key to life. When I went to school, they asked me what I wanted to be when I grew up. I wrote down 'happy'. They told me I didn't understand the assignment, and I told them they didn't understand life.

John Lennon

Introduction

Parenting is Really. Fucking. Hard. I know a fellow social worker who doesn't have any children of her own but investigates allegations of child abuse for her career. She would say this all the time: "if you're doing it right, it's going to be hard!" All too often, she would see parenting "from the couch" instead of hands-on, interactive and engaged parenting. If you are parenting, you are going to be tired, you are going to be frustrated, you're going to go to all the museums, watch all the cartoons, pick up all the Cheerios, dry all the tears, wash all the stains from the clothes. Some days are going to feel like you cannot go on one more second, and other days are going to be the most wonderful and memorable days of your life. You're going to go to bed in tears, and then wake up and do it all over again, coffee cup in hand. And even if you are getting up for the seventh time in the middle of the night to a fussy baby, you love them, dammit, you just love them and you'd get up seven more times if you had to.

7

This is going to be a tough journey; the reward is gigantic yet cannot be measured. I am writing this from a modern, Western perspective. When you live in this world, trying to parent like some of the more indigenous people do might not work in your environment. You aren't going to have the kind of support a small community might have. Contact with the outside world in a modern society is necessary when you live in modern society, and modern society is full of obstacles, and well, other overwhelmed parents.

While we are enthusiastically chugging away on auto-pilot parenting, there is one truth: Parenting skills can be learned. Wanting to learn and wanting to do things differently from your own parents is not a small thing – it is a revolutionary act. It is a treasonous act of outright rebellion. Often the way you were parented came from generations of knowledge and tradition. Sadly, I have heard parents tell a judge in family court more than once, "I parent the way my parents did me, and I turned out okay." Everyone just stares, incredulously, because it does not reflect well on you to be saying this in Family Court because you, in fact, did not take care of your child. So there will be parents who are compelled to change their ways and how they want to parent along with the volunteers.

There are also many parents out there who have read all the books, blogs, gone to seminars, have degrees in psychology or even pediatrics and they are *still* struggling. The "terrible 2s and 3s" don't care how much you know. Children come into their world with their personalities. If you are a pacifist, you could get a kid who is a natural-born fighter. If you are prone to argue, your child may just sit quietly and stare at you as you seethe. Kids are smart, but you are smarter. They won't remember what they were mad at you for when they wake up the next day, or after their nap. This is the time to get a handle on who is in charge, when they are little, not when they are older. I have to break it to you honestly: There is a strategy for turning things around with your parenting when they are teens, but if you can start much, much sooner, things will turn out better.

Starting down this road can lead you to have arguments with your family, can cause your friends' eyes to roll up far into their foreheads when you talk about your parenting – what you are doing, or planning to do – in order to raise the most perfect, loveable, smart and successful human ever created. So first, hold your horses, scale back on your grandiosity. The unknown variable here is your child. You have control over so much of your life, and so little all at the same time. You have even less control over other human beings, including who your child turns out to be. If your parents are world class singers who toured Europe in their college choir, that does not mean your child will be able to so much as carry a simple tune. Chances are they will, but that's not my point. You won't know your child's personality, skill set, temperament, preferences - until they do. You can read all the books but no single formula will apply to your child at every step of their life. Here is where your skills must come in. You need to know when to apply which tactic to which child... and it is overwhelming and it will be hard to know how to do those things when you're tired, upset, anxious, or distracted.

All my life, I have had a strong feeling that I would be good at parenting. I liked kids; it was as simple as that, and I always knew I wanted a couple of my own. I have a brother who was adopted the year before I was born, and a younger sister who also came along the usual way, like I did. I knew that I could do either or both when I decided to become a parent, in order to become a parent one day. Before I had any children, I babysat, a lot. That was my first job. I started with school aged kids and then started getting more work with younger children, including babies. I learned a lot about kids and about myself and I think often about the developmental milestones I got to witness, the worries when they got sick or scraped a knee, and the frustration I felt when they would refuse to listen to me because, "you're not my mom!" I can laugh about it all now, at least.

So- at the ripe age of 33 and then again at 36 I did become a parent and I now have two almost grown up girls who are both wonderful and as different as two people could be. I will be the first to tell you: it has not been an easy journey. Even if I thought I would know what to do, I didn't always know what to do. I had to examine some of my knee-jerk responses, things I was too lax about, my anxieties about the future, how I was letting the normal behaviors and events in my kids' lives trigger emotions that were about me and not them.

I want to write a book about parenting that is accessible. I want it to be helpful and enjoyable to parents who have a Ph.D. and parents who barely made it out of high school. This will not be a stodgy, academic type of read. All parents can raise a child to be a success, however that is defined. Out of all the people I have met who were "successful" in my work, I have to say that the common denominator was always love. Their parents loved them and did anything and everything to give them a good start in life and that was not cold hard cash money. It was love. These incredible people were a joy to their parents, were held to high standards of behavior and encouraged to follow their dreams. This book is not going to be chock full of mumbo-jumbo big words about neurons and scientific studies done on twins with a five point plan to ensure your child grows up to be a millionaire. Hell, I am barely going to add any actual research to support my claims just to prove how much I have read about it, because you probably don't want to read that stuff anyway. Or, maybe you already have.

You should also know that a lot of what I know is based on studies and other parenting books, as well as my own experiences. I'm not just making stuff up, I promise. I have been working with children and families since 1993, I have picked up a lot of knowledge since then. I will, however, provide you with some solid resources for you to find more of what you might need if you don't get it here. When you are done reading this, I want you to feel validated, empowered and armed with good, practical steps toward being a good parent, if not a better parent than you were before. I also hope you find this funny, but not in the sense that I am just going to be funny and not give you the information you are hoping for. This isn't exactly comedy and I probably won't say that a child is "an asshole" at any point. Yes, in case you were wondering, there is a book or two out there like that.

In early 2018 I started a self-help book club, even though I wasn't (yet) a big fan of the genre. I wanted to have a bigger presence in my neighborhood, meet new friends, and possibly learn some new things. To my surprise, I have learned a lot since then, including how someone goes into the self-help writing business. It seems like it would help to be able to talk about when I got sober – I am not in recovery. Meaning, I am not an alcoholic. No, I am not in denial, I promise. Women lately seem to tout how much wine they drink and even wear t-shirts about Chardonnay. That's just not me. But being able to write about how I overcame adversity to get to an enlightened state isn't going to be my approach. I have overcome a lot of adversity, certainly, and I had a lot of trials on my parenting journey, but nothing that I didn't feel equipped to handle. I grew up one of those people who was "always an adult," as one of my therapists observed about me. I had shitty things happen to me and around me, but I have somehow managed to keep my shit together and move forward despite it all.

Every day as a therapist, I work with parents who are struggling, and I share an insight or a strategy here and there and it just seems like I need to put them all into one place instead of dispersed like dandelion seeds. I can influence a lot more people this way. I am also not an online "influencer" who gathers up other people's insight and boxes it up for others using "y'all" and "girl" constantly to grab someone's attention and drive home a point. I am writing from the perspective of an expert in both learning and experience. I have spent time reading some of the comments and reviews of other parenting books and I have found that there is a concerning number of parents who do not feel they got what they needed from a book. I want to change that! I want everyone to strive toward having a better life; but the truth is, sometimes it may take a generation beyond ours to really reap the benefits. We are going to break a cycle we may not be around to see the results - but we can set so much into motion.

I also include some important concepts and values while parenting that I consider the most important. These are: respect, communication, empathy, accountability and relationship. Using these concepts throughout your journey through parenting children will enhance your child's ability to pass these on to the people in their lives, not just their own children. Children should be treated like they are important and worthy if we as parents are to have the expectation that they listen and follow our leads. This will include refraining from any use of physical punishment, even a "spanking" as so many of us experienced as children. The idea that someone who says they love us can also do us great harm lasts well into our adult lives, affects how we perceive the world and how we expect our loved ones to treat us as adults. It is not useful or helpful and it teaches kids that hitting and even violence can solve problems. That is a plain lie that we have been taught is truth.

It has been well documented that adults who commit a number of crimes often grew up in homes that lacked stability and nurturing. When interviewed, convicted adult criminals, sex offenders in particular, admit that they began many of their behaviors in childhood. They lacked empathetic parenting, communication and real accountability. Many of the solutions to these issues are kept within academia or the treatment environment and are not disseminated to the public, unless you have time to go researching on your own. Only when a family finds itself involved with the criminal justice or child welfare systems can some of these family dynamics be addressed. I believe this is a mistake; adult parents are capable of making small but significant changes in their parenting style that can address these deficits. Even "nice" families can end up with children who are abusive, so before you think, "that will never happen to me," take a deep breath and hold onto that thought for a bit longer.

In the past few years there have been some pretty high-profile sexual assault cases where a young man is treated differently because he came from a "nice" family. Even in the case where the offender was caught in the act, he was given leniency and justifications by the criminal justice system as well as his parents, as made in statements to the media. I am not going to name these people; their names are already too well known. I can easily see how the dismissive responses of both the parents and the judicial system reinforced behaviors by the offender. Without accountability, nothing will change. And all of the people involved, including and especially the victim, were from "nice" families.

This book will be broken down by age group starting with getting knocked up or finding that the stork brought you a small human while you slept. No matter how you got your child, you're going to have to parent it. Then we'll move up the development scale into toddlerdom, or the Age of Tyranny as I like to call it. These little people are in tune with their power and aren't afraid to use it. But they need you all the same to chase away the monsters and to kiss all the boo-boos. School-aged kids are challenging and fun – they have friends and activities and suddenly decide they won't eat another vegetable ever again. Pre-teens and teens are practically another species but somehow, if we are reading this, we made it through ourselves and so will your child(ren). Tough times will be ahead, and I include some good tactics to handle those, don't worry. You are going to launch some awesome people out into the world, *yes you are!*

While the concepts I discuss here can be applied to most children, including those kids who have special needs; this isn't a book specifically about kids with special needs. There are so many specific and varied kinds of needs and diagnoses out there that I would have to write an encyclopedia instead of a guide. Autism, Cerebral Palsy, behavior and mood disorders, chronic illness, learning disabilities, trauma, foster care placement and on and on. I can't address all of those parenting needs and there are lots of specialized books for your particular situation out there. That is another reason I am including a resource section at the end to help you find what you might need to parent your particular kid, who is as unique and wonderful as each grain of sand at the beach. *Awww...*

I have been impressed with my same age peers that I grew up with; we were all "latch key kids" of baby boomer era, Woodstock hippie, Me Generation parents. We were mostly on our own, figuring it out, sometimes failing, sometimes succeeding, wondering if we were ever good enough. Looking at how they (and I) have chosen to parent has been astonishing. We have all endeavored to be involved! To aspire to raise kids who have a relationship with us and vice versa. And so many of them are doing great. After each chapter I am going to pose a few questions for you to reflect on. You can write them down or reflect on them as you drive to work, but I suggest you do a little writing so you can record your nuggets of insight and ideas about your plans and solutions to your parenting dilemmas.

I also want to stress that it is less important about *what* your child grows up to do than *who* they want to be. You can set all the goals you like – what school they'll attend, how many languages they'll speak, what career they get into and how much money they'll earn. None of that is within your power. Like John Lennon, I have always said I just want my kids to be happy. If they are happy, they will follow their own dreams and everything they want or need will fall into place.

Recently in the news a scandal broke where several actors and other wealthy parents were caught bribing college staff to help get their child into a school. In at least one case, the child wasn't even attending classes. Not only was the parent's behavior unethical, but it is just bad parenting. Their child was perfectly happy and following her dreams successfully without even attending college. The scandal caused the child to lose all of their already in place and lucrative business prospects. It just makes no sense! Especially when the bribes cost more than four years of tuition! I'm not saying anything that hasn't already been said on this topic, I'm just still dumbstruck by it. My daughters brought it up to me in front of the grocery store magazine rack and felt the same way. They intend to get good grades to go to a college they'd like to attend, make friends, move out on their own, and earn a living. They don't know exactly how just yet, they just know that they have the ability to accomplish this. That's all I can ask for.

The sign of great parenting is not the child's behavior.
The sign of truly great parenting is the parent's
behavior.

-Andy Smithson

Chapter 1

Parenting is a skill

Since the days of Dr. Spock's baby bible, <u>The Common Sense Book About Baby and Child Care</u> (1946), about a million books on parenting and how-to parent have been written, and a good number before that were in circulation for generations, believe it or not. Parents have also turned to their elders from the dawn of time to ask advice on everything from how to care for a newborn baby to how to deal with a teenager who insists on learning the hard way. We learn from our experiences growing up as well, our parents learned from their parents, and so on. Most of us just do what we know, good or bad, until all those darn books came out of course! Now we have to contend with not only the advice of our parents, our in-laws, siblings, neighbors, kindly strangers at the grocery store on how to parent our kids, but all of those so-called "experts" out there who believe they have found the Holy Grail to making parenting easier. As if one size really fits all.

As it turns out, much of the information that has been taken as gospel for parents over the generations, is anecdotal. There are very few actual scientific studies available that have tested the various theories or styles. A writer in the 1980's named Christina Hardyment discovered after reading all of the books, 650 to be exact, that most of the information was based on some pretty un-scientific information. She also highlighted the fact that parenting trends can flip flop from year to year – the things we took for truth turned out to be not such good advice after all. Well, that's great, now what do we do? I for one, think that every human is different from the other, and sometimes experiencing a challenge in life makes us not only interesting, but even more unique, compassionate and open (or closed) to ideas; we pass this down to our children through our parenting style no matter how many books we have read.

There are all kinds of skills that can be learned. This can be woodworking, or drawing (yes anyone can learn to draw but talent helps, just as in woodworking), or swimming, or solving mathematical equations. Going on to higher levels of these, like framing a house, competing in the Olympics or getting a Ph.D. in math is a choice, and if you are doing something you love, it won't be a tough decision to make. Parenting is the same way – you have chosen to raise a child and should therefore get as good at is as you can as though you were going for your doctoral degree at the University of Life. Parenting is not passive, the word itself is both a noun and a verb. It is an active word – it is something you must be awake and oriented to do. Learn all you can, practice, read up, discuss issues with other parents and brainstorm solutions. Make it your purpose on a daily basis to show love and respect to your child/children, teach them to communicate their needs, have empathy for others, take accountability for mistakes and be in relationship with you. You do this by doing this with them and with the adults you interact with.

I've heard people say that they're going to get a dog to prepare them for parenting. I also once had a client who needed help with parenting and rejected a therapist who told her, "I'm not a parent, but I have a dog." Parenting is not the same as having a pet. Animals have simpler brains, might be naughty sometimes but generally adore their people and do whatever they can to be adored back. You have to be responsible and feed them, walk them, clean up their messes and take them to the vet when they need shots or get sick. Similarly, you don't leave them in a hot car or go on vacation with no one looking after them for days at a time. But that is where the similarities end. Human children start off being completely dependent on an adult human to survive, and this lasts for several years. Knowing this is helpful, as knowing all stages of child development is helpful to this journey. We all need to know what realistic expectations are for children.

In today's climate, there is more to worry about than ever before. Our kids are doing active shooter drills in Kindergarten for Pete's sake; however, my parents recall doing nuclear annihilation drills while hiding under their desks. No-one realized during the cold war how stressful this might be on our children and on the parents. People were taught to believe that they would survive the bombs this way: hiding in school and in personal or public bomb shelters. We worry about all kinds of tragedies striking our families, even and most especially when things are going well. We are trained to believe that if things are good, something wicked will be coming our way to ruin everything. This idea blends into the topic of parenting while having a diagnosed condition such as anxiety or depression while having to be an engaged and interactive parent. Stress, while something that we can manage, is temporary while mental illness might need some ongoing management. We also have to be able to address our children's stress as well as our own.

When you have a baby, your ability to regulate your emotions will affect your baby's ability to regulate their emotions. Babies literally "feed" off their parents through their skin-to-skin contact. If you are nervous and breathing hard, babies feel that and learn to feel unsafe. Alternately, when you are calm and you hug your frightened child, they learn to take physical contact as a way to self soothe and will seek you out. If you are too depressed to respond to a crying baby in the crib, the baby will become depressed, stop crying and learn not to ask for what they need. If you are a parent who expects a child to get only A's in school, that child will learn to please you but not to enjoy learning new things and have feelings of accomplishment. If you are critical of your teen's fashion choices, that teen will not feel they are able to express themselves openly and hide their true selves from you. Make no mistake, the stakes are high.

We can royally screw our kids up, and we might anyway. The point is, this book will help you do your best and your best will be good enough.

You can still be a good parent if you are struggling to manage stress, anxiety, depression, PTSD, or bipolar among other things. If you decide to take medication, that's your decision and a surprising number of parents do. Find some support from other parents who are going through something similar or having support from a relative or friend nearby. Having social contacts who know you and support you is another very effective way to prevent child abuse and neglect.

If you find yourself surrounded by judgement, check your own self-compassion – do you feel bad for being who you are? Stand tall, you're making an informed choice to take care of your health as well as your mental health. You have a child, and you're too important to them to be unhappy. If you are struggling with substance abuse, even that nightly bottle or two of wine: seek help. Many Alcoholics Anonymous groups have groups for parents so children are welcome. Marijuana is also becoming increasingly legal and may soon be legal throughout the United States. Heavy use during parenting is a hindrance to good parenting, just as alcohol is a hindrance. There are also services out there to take advantage of before you lose the choice. Parenting under the influence is not real parenting. You may not realize it but your kids may instead be parenting you, and they will resent you for that forever. Guilt trip much? Yes, if it helps you get it together.

Control is going to be a buzzword. We can't control everything but we can control a lot: our routines, our kids' general routines, precautions such as wearing a seatbelt, using a car seat for the kids, looking both ways before crossing the street, our use of birth control to avoid becoming parents in the first place. You get the idea. You also cannot control your child. This is one of the Western styles that has been promoted throughout the culture – we should *control* their behavior, when they eat, when they sleep. I believe this just sets parents up for constant friction. Being able to distinguish between what we can control and what we cannot control can go a long way. The way we explain these worries to kids and what we can control vs not control will help them manage their fears in turn. For example:

> Child comes home: Mom, today we had a fire drill.
>
> Mom: oh yeah? How did that go?
>
> Child: I was scared we had a real fire.
>
> Mom: Was there a real fire?
>
> Child: No, but the firetrucks came so that was cool.
>
> Mom: yes, firetrucks are cool.
>
> Child: What if we do have a real fire?
>
> Mom: You will follow the class out of the school to get to safety, just like you practiced. You

might still get scared, but you have a plan and that's important.

The key parenting skill? Relationship. We have relationships with all kinds of people but this is going to be a big one. When they are little, the relationship is through touch, voice, tone, routine. As they grow, you have to get to know them, listen to their fears, validate them, encourage them. Did I mention listen? Yes, for those of you sitting in the back – LISTEN to your kids. When they know you can hear and accept their worries, dreams, plans without losing your mind with boredom, horror, anxiety, they will pretty much tell you anything and everything even when they are teenagers. You heard me; I'm not making this up.

If we jump into our conclusions too fast, we can quickly spoil a chance to get to know our child. "you were scared of a little fire drill? They're no big deal, why, when I was a kid..." Or "Maybe someday you will be a firefighter and ride one of those trucks, wouldn't that be cool?" You can drive that conversational firetruck right off a cliff this way. Be curious, ask questions. Play dumb like you have no idea what your child is talking about (even if you think you do). Let your child talk, explore thoughts, help them with new words, like for feelings they can't explain yet. Make eye contact, smile and do other non-verbal engagement signs, like leaning toward them. Pretend they are a person you'd like to get to know better at a party. They are evolving a little bit more every day and you are their greatest teacher. I know this is a monster-sized cliché that is so overused I could not even begin to find a citation for but it's true so let's accept it and move on.

When my second daughter, Olivia, was 6, I signed her up to do an introductory class in her sister's cheerleading group. I never grew up with a cheerleading and sports culture in New York City; so it seemed silly to me. But my older daughter was having fun and getting exercise and my younger daughter wanted to do something as well. Ten minutes into the routine, and my little, sassy, sarcastic blonde child looked over at me and mouthed, "this is stupid." I fell in love with her in that moment for the thousandth time. *That's my girl*. Instead, about a week later, she asked to join the after school karate program that would run for about 6 weeks. She is now working toward her second degree black belt in Taekwondo (we switched early on, long story). She loves martial arts and has a good feel for it. My older child left cheerleading shortly after and pursues her own interests as well. I'm fortunate that I have been able to send my kids to classes; and that we had inexpensive options near us. We made it happen the best way we could because Olivia made a decision and Olivia followed through with it.

As I was explaining this book concept to an old friend, she posed an interesting question: Do you think that you can tell a parent how to parent better if you haven't gone through the same issues that they have? I'll be honest, I have been asked this question many times, about many subjects. My answer is generally the same. If you are a parent who is struggling, and at the same time you are pushing back on the people who know different from you, then do you truly want the help? I am not saying that I know everything and all about parenting every child.

What I know is *different* from what you know and if you are open to receiving new and helpful information, then you will do better. If you are oppositional and closed off, your child will be mirroring you at home. How on earth can one person know about every child out there? We can't! You have to be the expert on your child and partner with the helpers involved with your family – your pediatrician, a therapist, teachers, who know information that can help you. Please keep an open mind and heart as you go through your parenting journey.

Summary

1. Build your relationship over time, tune in
2. Be curious, ask questions
3. Listen, listen and listen some more

Now You:

1. List 3-5 parenting styles or skills you grew up with that you'd like to keep as a parent?

2. List 3-5 parenting styles or skills you grew up with that you want to lose as a parent?

3. List 3-5 questions you have about being a parent that you hope to have answered by the end of this book.

4. List 5 ways you are building a relationship with your child.

"All those clichés, those things you hear about having a baby and motherhood—all of them are true. And all of them are the most beautiful things you will ever experience."

-Penelope Cruz

Chapter 2

So You Have this Baby... Now What?

F amilies are made in a couple of ways – someone gets pregnant, and someone or a couple of someone's get to parent the baby. Sometimes it is a person who did not biologically create this life form and chose to raise it anyway. Let's face it, babies are pretty cute, whether or not they look anything like you. You'll need an open heart and a lot of patience. You'll cherish the pouty, drooly, snuggly moments and in the same day wonder what you were thinking taking this on. It's a confusing place to live in until you get the hang of it; and then your child moves on to a new phase of development and you're starting over. In a nutshell, a baby:

AGE	MILESTONE
1-3 months	Makes eye contact, makes a fist, has a specific cry for each need (food, change, holding), smiles, coos, drools, poops a lot, sleeps 18-12 hours per day.

3-6 months	Rolls over, more complex vocalizations, giggles, holds body up better, "stands" in your lap, might get a first tooth.
6-9 months	Sits up, scoots around on their belly, pulls up to stand holding furniture, begins soft solid foods,
9-12 months	Crawls, cruises around the furniture while holding on, maybe takes first steps, uses a push-walker, says a word, eats more textured solid foods, uses hands to eat, holds own bottle/cup. Fewer naps, might sleep most of the night if not all night.

Knowing what to expect from your baby will help you be patient and not freak out when they aren't yet speaking in full sentences by six months. It is also well documented that knowing child development can prevent child abuse, and who doesn't want that? This first year is the biggest growth and learning year of their lives, and while we see all kinds of videos of first steps, the other milestones are just as exciting.

Now I have mentioned respect, communication, empathy, accountability and relationship as the most important factors in parenting. How are these applied to a teeny-tiny baby, you ask? Well, I'm going to tell you. First of all, you have a natural instinct to respond to your baby. That is so far into our DNA since the days we were all protoplasmic algae bubbling near some volcano a million or three years ago. Most of us struggle to hear a baby cry for too long – we long to go to it and pick it up.

When a cat is outside howling and it sounds like a baby, we go out to be sure it's just a cat. Even then, many of us would want to find that cat and make sure it is okay. As animals ourselves, we can't help it. Responding to a baby who is hungry is a form of respect toward your baby. They are not trying to control you or manipulate you into doing their bidding. They're just hungry and they know you are going to come through. You might not think I need to say this, but yes, there are still people who are taught that babies are trying to manipulate adults.

With your touch and tone of voice, you communicate to your baby that everything is going to be okay. You sing to them, rock them, burp them after a feeding because they are fussy and they are telling you that they need it. You are tuning in to how they communicate. It is usually by crying, but after a while, this conversation gets more and more intricate. If your baby is hungry, he or she will turn her head and open his or her mouth; they may also start getting wiggly or antsy. Waiting until they cry is too late; they are mad now because they've been telling you that they want food and you missed it. No judgement, now you know, and you try again because the baby will be hungry again and again.

Empathy is your ability to feel and sense the feelings of another person. This kind of sixth sense will help you also be a better parent, and comes more in handy as the years go by. We'll also look closer at holding your child accountable, but at this age, can they really do anything wrong? *No, no they can't, because they're so cute. Yes they are.* FYI, baby talk is great for babies. But only for babies. Remember to talk like an adult when you go out with your peers or speak up in a meeting at work.

Babies are good little travelers as well. They are happiest when they are with you and physically close to you, as when you are carrying them. Since ancient times, women at least, have done their daily tasks with babies wrapped around them with colorful cloths, or baskets, and boards. Ideally, there is little barrier between the bodies, because I have said, they can self-regulate based on another person's regulating. This is also important while sleeping. Babies brains are quite primitive, but being close to someone who is breathing steadily and is warm, helps their brains learn to keep on ticking. Babywearing isn't controversial but co-sleeping is. When safe, co-sleeping is a great way for everyone to get their sleep and be happy. Why shouldn't a baby be happy? Nursing mothers can even nurse in their sleep or while walking along with a baby wrapped up against her. Those car seats people carry around are heavy, too. They are meant for cars; they are hard backed and angled for safety in a vehicle. If ever you can, pick up the baby and transfer him or her to a sling or body carrier.

Why is co-sleeping controversial? When we observe other mammals in the wild, we see them sleeping piled up in a cave, tree trunk, nest, happily snoozing away. Gorillas don't put their babies down and go sleep next to another tree. Everyone is happiest when sleeping near one another. Sadly, Sudden Infant Death Syndrome (SIDS) is a real worry. It is a risk for young infants because their neurology is not fully developed, among other reasons. According to the Centers for Disease Control, since the introduction of the Safe to Sleep campaign in 1994, rates of SIDS have dropped dramatically. This tells us that there are things you can do to lower your child's risks such as not smoking, not drinking or using any drugs while co-sleeping, use light blankets for yourself and none for the baby, just a warm pajama set. Overlaying a baby while fast asleep can kill a baby or do great harm because the baby can lose oxygen to the brain for too long resulting in brain damage. You need to take precautions and ultimately make a decision that works for your family, not what everyone else is doing.

Baby carrier slings, car seats, cribs, bottle warmers, strollers… there is more gear in baby-land than any other time of life. There are diaper bags marketed just to the "cool dads" who want to be seen in public with their baby, but not with a powder pink princess diaper bag over their shoulder. You are told that you "need" all this stuff when you have a baby, and of course you "need" the most expensive, top of the line, and trendy stuff. That's garbage. While some of the gear is necessary, there is a lot that we never end up using. Most expecting parents don't have money to buy all of this stuff, so I always recommend having a baby shower. They can be kept simple, but I think it is the best idea ever brought to light; everyone gets the things they need for their baby, and no one person has to buy all of it at once. It's a wonderful way for us to take care of each other. More than that, we can often use the gear for the (gasp!) next baby. Or pass it on to a friend as long as there are no safety recalls or damages to the product.

Attachment and Bonding

This phase of human development is critical to babies because it also involves bonding. The concept of bonding isn't new to humans, and it has been researched since the 1960s with the studies by psychologist John Bowlby on attachment. There is an entire parenting style called Attachment Parenting promoted primarily by pediatrician Dr. William Sears. It means that wherever we go, the baby goes. We engage the baby, make eye contact while feeding and talking with the baby; we sleep with or near the baby and the baby in turn sees us, the parents, as an extension of its own body. There is clear communication between the two bodies and the baby's needs are primary even if mom or dad doesn't want to get up one more time. This style is thought of as more of a "hippie" style for some reason – when we see a colorful baby sling on a woman with long hair who is nursing a baby and a toddler, perhaps? Know that there is so much judgement on how you choose to parent, no matter how you choose to parent. That "hippie" parent? She's judging you right back, by the way.

Another important discovery was made during this time by researcher Henry Harlow using baby rhesus monkeys. These babies were removed from their mothers and raised with either a wire monkey mother or a furry mother substitute. The babies with a wire substitute showed very serious behavior problems, as compared with the ones who had a soft, cuddly, substitute, and would eventually shut down psychologically. Giving food and shelter are the very bare minimum for animals and humans alike; giving love is essential for complete human development. If anyone comments that you are "holding the baby too much," and "spoiling your baby," remember these little monkeys, who thankfully no longer have to be used in experiments like these.

During graduate school I worked with teen mothers in a group home. One mother was watching her baby while he was in his stroller. I asked her why she did not pick him up? She said, "The staff in the daycare tell us not to hold the babies too much because during the day they don't have time to be holding our kids," but this young woman clearly longed to pick her son up. I asked her a question: "if the staff isn't holding your baby, and you aren't holding your baby, when is anyone holding your baby?" She looked at me quickly with an understanding in her eyes and then, reached down and picked him up. I later discussed this with the director of the department who said she would address that issue with all of their group homes. These babies were already in a high-risk category, why make it worse?

Boundaries

Being able to set strong boundaries with people who would judge will make life easier. A simple Google search of the word BOUNDARIES gives us this definition:

> Personal boundaries are guidelines, rules or limits that a person creates to identify reasonable, safe and permissible ways for other people to behave towards them and how they will respond when someone passes those limits.

You may have a mother in law who doesn't understand nursing or vice versa and lectures you on the merits of "how she did it," and even put you down for how you are choosing to feed your child. The playground is another place that is supposed to be fun and where you meet other parents, but you will find parents judging one another just as quickly. They judge what they cannot control, what is making them anxious, not because of anything you are doing. What do you do when you are confronted with judgements and pressure to conform to someone else's philosophy – and let's just assume you are not doing anything dangerous like trying to make a vegan baby formula in your kitchen or leaving the baby with the dog while you go to the grocery store. Here are some examples:

> **Judgement:** Are you going to breastfeed that baby forever? It can't be good for them.

> **Boundary:** I am choosing what I think is best for my baby. You don't have to agree.

> **Judgement:** But people can see your breasts and what will other children think?

> **Boundary:** They will see a mother feeding a baby. Children don't associate it with something sexual. Please stop making these hurtful

36

comments to me; I am enjoying my baby and being a parent and I don't appreciate being judged.

Some other, less diplomatic, responses could be: *Shut up, leave me the fuck alone, mind your own damn business.* It will really depend on who is doing the judging and whether or not you want to continue having a relationship with that person. Set your boundaries like a boss in any case. There are going to be a lot of choices you'll have to make as a parent, feeding being only one. You'll decide if you want an Obstetrician or a Midwife for delivery (and all the birth details), if you'll need to go back to work, what kind of child care will work for your family, cloth or plastic diapers, brand of stroller, which Pediatrician to see, color scheme in the baby's room, and so on until you've sent the kid off to college and perhaps beyond. You don't have to share or defend your *reasonable parenting decisions* to anyone. Got that?

I was recently out in the community and observed a young mother, her toddler, and the grandmother. The mother had her child in the stroller and was giving the toddler a juice box back and forth. The grandmother started berating her daughter, the young mother, "why are you giving her juice? She's not thirsty, where are you gonna take her to the bathroom?" The mother then snatches the bottle away and starts to seem irritated. The more the grandmother commented and overrode her daughter's parenting, the more irritated the young mother became and at one point, swatted her toddler's hand as the child reached back for the box of juice. Their voices became very similar when speaking to their respective children. This was a good example for me to use in my writing, however, not a good example of how to not let someone get under your skin about how you choose to parent. Another example comes from many years ago while I was having a vacation at Lake George, New York. While I was on the dock, another family was floating on the dock and had several children, aged approximately two to ten with two or three between them. The toddler took a swipe at a sibling, the ten-year-old slapped the toddler's hand, and the mother slapped the ten-year-old's hand and said, "stop hitting, where do you think he gets that?" It was all I could do to keep my mouth shut. It was the classic pecking order from my college textbooks come to life.

In times of stress, and you will have these times, what will you do to stay safe and sane? If you aren't able to find balance for having a life with your baby and having some time to recharge your batteries, you are going to burn right out and be left in the dark wondering what to do to get the lights turned back on. As I have stressed earlier, hitting only creates more hitting. Not every child who was hit will hit their children, but it takes a toll long term on their mental health. You love your baby but if you don't take some time away, the results won't be good. And a word to the fathers, or otherwise the parent who isn't the primary caregiver: Don't be a selfish asshole. Make sure your partner has the opportunity and time to recharge. Take the baby and send them to a long, hot shower. Do the laundry, clean the house and pick up groceries on the way home. Caring for a baby is hard work and it doesn't last forever. Expecting them to behave as if nothing had changed is insane and you might deserve to be sent to the couch to sleep on from now on.

Couples

Having a baby is going to impact your relationship, no matter what you do. Nothing is going to be the same; and as I wrote above, you cannot expect your post-partum partner to get back on track as if they didn't just go through the biggest physical shock of their lives. They might look okay but they are still recovering. I hear all too often that the non-child bearing parent feels shut out of the intense dyad that is mother and baby. They want all the things that the baby has: the attention, the love, the closeness, the nursing, to be the complete center of the universe. Perhaps we all have some left-over memories of when we were infants that is creating this yearning? I'm not sure how science could figure that one out, but I know that parents, specifically dads, need to knock that shit off.

Your job, as the one who didn't grow a human being in your body and push it out a small opening after the cramps from hell, is to take care of the woman who did. She is scared, vulnerable, in pain, exhausted and hormonal. She feels like a deflated hot air balloon, sore and tender all over and probably just wants her mommy, not a man who keeps talking about how happy he will be when her six-week checkup reveals she is "ready" to have sex again. So go take a cold shower and have a seat.

Scratch that, don't take a seat, get off your ass and do your part.

What do women need after giving birth? They need to drink water, especially if they are nursing, so fill up the pitcher and keep it full for her; make her a sandwich while you are at it. They need to be able to get to the bathroom to change their post birth maxi to-the-max pads, disposable maternity underwear and coat herself with witch hazel wipes. Make sure she isn't sitting in her rocker all night long because the baby cries every time she tries to put the baby down to go pee. She needs to be able to shower to wash all that muck off herself, her own as well as the baby's spit up and poop.

She could use a long back rub with no ulterior motives because her back hurts. She needs to be taken to a maternity store for new bras, she needs to be able to catch up on her sleep while you tend the baby with no resentment; and finally she needs to be told she is a radiant goddess who is doing a beautiful job being a mother while having tears and hearts in your eyes, not told she's "doing it all wrong," and "you and the baby kept me up all night!" yes those are real quotes. Horrified? Good. This should be a beautiful, happy time in family's life, and giving the right support at the right time will help to make that happen.

Not all men were raised to accept more modern gender roles, so this may be hard for some new fathers. These may also be the dads who carry the diaper bags for cool dudes, I'm not sure. Gender roles play a large part in how much initiative parents take when babies come along.

There are the dads who are jealous of the mother who can breastfeed, and there are dads who want nothing to do with the messy life that is caring for a baby, but who later want to teach their sons how to throw a ball. You child may not want to throw a ball, did you think of that? Or you could teach your daughter how to fix engines on the weekend. As I have said, I have been impressed with a lot of my peers from childhood who are very involved parents, men and women. So I am hoping that there is less and less rigidity in how most men approach their new role as parent. Women are tough bad-asses for giving birth, can men also be tough bad-asses for being gentle and loving? I think so.

Sleep

Speaking of sleep, the biggest, baddest topic on every parent forum on the Web, everyone wants to discover the fool proof way to get babies and kids to fall asleep the second they are put down on the bed. Sorry, fools, there isn't one way to do this. Some parents swear by "nursing down" at night, some walk and pace the floors, some babies go to sleep after some fussing in the crib. Babies don't know what time it is so they need to be taught, conditioned, to go to sleep at a certain time. For this you need a routine. Do you remember learning about the Russian behaviorist, Anton Pavlov? He paired a ringing bell with feeding time for his dogs to elicit the drooling response. Producing saliva is a biological response to prepare to break down food for digestion. Once conditioned, the dogs only needed a bell sound to begin drooling, whether or not they were fed. Similarly, sleep is a biological response to fatigue. Our bodies and brains need to rest for optimal health, and young babies need more than everyone. So when we pair the babies routine with the time for sleep, babies learn to sleep. My routine was as follows: Warm bath or face wash, clean diaper, jammies, dark room, music box, nursing and rocking. Did the baby fall right to sleep? Sometimes. Again, remember what I said in the beginning: parenting is hard. But this routine worked for me. It also sent me right to sleep because, remember, I was in the room doing the routine too!

The band, The Talking Heads, wrote the lyric: *Baby baby, please let me hold you. I wanna make you stay up all night.* Babies are definitely cute and fun but you do not want to make staying up all night your routine. Find a routine that fits into your life and stick to it if it works, generally. Being clueless and staying up as long as the baby takes to fall asleep isn't going to be good for anyone. Getting up and turning on the lights and being entertaining as if it were broad daylight signals that nighttime is playtime. When babies wake up in the middle of the night, they need a new diaper, usually, and to be fed. The lights stay out, the room stays quiet. The babies are put back down to sleep. When it is light out, then you can signal to them that sleeping time is over. They are smart, and again, we are smarter.

So why is there no single way to do this stuff? Well, babies are all different. Mine is different from yours and all the other babies around the world. They have personalities woven into their DNA that hasn't fully emerged. You can see some of it now, but they can't really express themselves just yet. Oh if babies could talk... oh wait. They will talk some day! It is so easy to have expectations based on what we want, hope for, and believe. A lot of who they are will of course be similar to the parents, due to DNA, unless they aren't of your DNA. That makes the mystery even more – well – mysterious. Love is the factor that matters. When you show love, respect, routine, bonding, the babies will flourish to become who they are meant to become and we all just need to be patient with them.

Because life is chock full of all kinds of adversity and roadblocks, no matter how awesome you are, there will be scary times with your baby. You may be woken up in the middle of the night to find your child running a fever and wheezing; or vomiting like that poor girl in The Exorcist (thought it might not be green), or they rolled off a bed and that sickening *"ker-chunk"* sounds as they land on the hard floor. Perhaps you are seeing some developmental changes that seem regressed, or that they aren't making gains as expected. These are all very likely scenarios. Chances are, your insurance or doctor's office has a Nurse Line or on-call line for questions like, "should I bring my baby to the ER?" If you are ever in doubt, just go in, either to the office or to the ER.

You know your baby better than anyone and you know if something is seriously wrong, even if you can't diagnose it yourself. These are scary experiences, and while you haven't had your baby for very long, you are quite attached and can't imagine life without them. Taking action is the best path to take, ignoring potential problems because you don't think you can handle the reality will land you in hot water, and potentially make your worst fears come true. If the worst-case scenario does come true, get support as soon as you can and for as long as you need it. I know too many parents who lost their babies young for a number of completely random and uncontrollable reasons. I'm not going to list any because you probably have already imagined most of them already in your anxious parenting moments. It is devastating and has a lasting impact for you and your family.

Summary:

1. Babies are cute and deserve your full attention and respect.
2. There is no such thing as too much love and holding for a baby.
3. You will be judged for all kinds of decisions you make about parenting.
4. A solid routine for baby care and trusting your instincts will make things easier.

Now You:

1. List 3 things that having a baby has changed about you.
2. List 3 things you need from your partner or family to help you survive this stage.

3. List 3 things you thought would happen and then the 3 things that happened instead after having a baby.

Having a two-year-old is like owning a blender that you don't have a top for."

-Jerry Sienfeld

Chapter 3

The Toddler – What Could Go Wrong?

By this time, your child will have taken some first steps and just like that moved from being an infant to a young toddler. They've got that big head to carry around now and just seem to be bumping into everything, accelerating their speech and language, wanting to be more independent at times, but still looking very much like a baby and have not quite started being what adults see as "manipulative." How much cuter could they be? For me, this age is a favorite time because of the above reasons. Here are some milestones in the toddler stage of human life. And for the record, parents and other professionals do count months until kids are around 3 years old because each month really can be quite different, developmentally and it helps to keep track this way:

AGE	MILESTONE
12-18 months	Walking, running, gibberish speech, understanding simple instructions,

	sleeping more consistently at night, first molars emerge (painful), inquisitive, want to look at books and play with toys, play with other children side by side (Not interactive), feeding self with utensils (still messy).
18-24 months	Wants more independence, improving speech and language, vocabulary is growing, showing some preference for taste, mimic adults, dancing to the beat of music, will show interest in using a toilet vs diapers.
24-30 months	Toilet training, two-year-old molars emerge (painful), first dental checkup, climbing, interested in friends, down to one nap per day, wants to be independent but also able to see caregiver nearby.
30-36 months	May trigger parents deliberately by saying "no," making up excuses to not go to sleep (I'm hungry), may run off suddenly, speaking in mostly full sentences, they can make simple choices.

The latter two phases tend to be the most upsetting to parents. As I have said, even some of the smartest and most loving parents are sent into a spiral of shame, worry, frustration and anger by some of their toddlers' behaviors. As if toddlers are doing it on purpose. They always want to push the elevator buttons, and you'll be stopping on every floor of every building if you don't stop them. Similarly, they will push all of your buttons the second they discover where they are. If making a mess makes a parent anxious... they will dump all their toys out and watch for your reaction. If noises from their toys – songs, beeps, sirens good lord make it stop... they will go around and turn them all on at the same time just to see you do the rock yourself with your hands over your ears. As adults, we see a little sociopath who we imagine will end up in prison one day. Not the case, thankfully! They are learning – they are social creatures who are learning to read social cues. How can you handle this?

Take a deep breath and smile at them. Narrate their play for them: "Oh now you are turning on all the songs at the same time." "You are dancing to all that music," "You just spilled out all the toys from the basket." There are no suggestions to make or questions to ask. You are showing them that you are paying attention to them but you are not reacting to them as if they are doing something bad to YOU. When it is time for quiet, we tell them, "in 10 seconds (count it down), it will be quiet time, let's let all the toys go night night..." and "It is time to pick up, let's see how fast we can get all the toys back in the basket." Anything you can make a game out of – do that. And if messes make you batty, you're getting your living room picked up. If they begin to fuss and cry, it may be too late for them to happily participate. Don't fight it, just scoop them up and move into the nap time routine. Just as when they were infants, toddlers will show signs of being tired, hungry, needing to poop, etc. You are learning their cues as well.

Talking to your baby and toddler is critical to their development of language. They will first learn to understand you, and they will try to mimic you with noises. What I see frequently, is that parents hear their baby make noises and think, "uh oh, my baby is about to cry in this crowded elevator" and they respond, "ssssshhhhhh." They try to get their babies to stop making noises. So… here's the problem with that. When we do that, we are telling them not to talk, not to try to communicate, not to be a nuisance, not to have a voice. That becomes our interaction. When a baby "talks," treat it like a conversation. "Oh yeah? Tell me all about it. And what else happened? Oh my goodness that sounds like fun," and so on. You are tuning in and developing your interaction and relationship and you can start this on Day One.

I think that we could talk for years about the toddler, and how their raw and unpredictable emotions drive most parents up a wall on a daily basis. They are just learning to express feelings and regulate themselves; as well as identify when they are tired, hungry, sad, scared. Feelings can feel too big for them and as parents we can't fall into a trap where we are Their Victims. Parents need to help them put words to their feelings and have some compassion for them. This is a short phase in their long lives and learning those good skills now will set the stage for them to enter childhood.

Now back to that "up the wall" thing. How do you know when you are getting to your limit? How do you prevent losing your shit with this little button pusher? Because, you really have to. Again, it's not about them, you are the one being triggered. Do you know why? Do you have the skills to regulate yourself? Same goes for you- name your feelings. Take your naps, take your deep breaths, do things you enjoy, find support, get some exercise. Take care of yourself too.

I certainly know that there are toddlers who cannot be left unattended for 30 seconds because they'll be into something. I've also seen a number of compilations online of kids doing all kinds of Naughty Behavior and wondered, "what were the parents doing when this was going on?" Yes, even I judge and I know that it only takes a moment to be using the bathroom or making lunch to realize, *it is way too quiet...* and boom! Because of this phenomenon, you are going to feel like you have no life to yourself. Reality check: You don't. At least not for a few more years. Before I had children, I was an avid painter, as you might have read in my biography. After children I didn't paint for five years. Then, after I remembered myself, and what I used to do for fun, I started painting again and it was a bit of a creative explosion. What I am trying to tell you is: there is hope, I promise. Your child will grow up and need less line-of-sight supervision and you'll notice it at first, and then forget what life used to be like, looking back wistfully at photos and wonder where that little angel went. Unless you decided to have another.

Second Baby

What? You didn't get enough the first time around? Here we go again, then. And this time, you have even more to juggle and kids can be competitive. Many of us think it might be obvious that you should try to explain what a sibling is to your first child in a way that is appropriate to their age and stage of development. Just in case it is not obvious, I am going to put it here. Kids need preparation, as much as you can give them. Sometimes, you don't have a lot of time, as when you are looking to adopt. You don't always know when that big day might come; but if mom's belly is getting bigger and bigger, you can use that as a jumping off point for discussion. Older siblings want to feel special, they want to be included, they have no idea what is about to happen to their happy life as an older child. I distinctly recall moments with my children, when daddy would comment baby talk to the new baby and the older child would begin to whine. At first it was the knee jerk response to tell the older girl not to whine. But when we looked carefully, there was a pattern to this. I mentioned this one day and it was clear – any attention given to the baby created a whiny, sad sound from the toddler.

I even came home from work one day, greeted the toddler and reached for the baby. My toddler body-blocked me, open armed and panting with wild eyes as she prevented me from getting closer to the baby who was in the arms of their babysitter. Instead, I reached down and picked up my first girl and spent some time with her asking about her day. The next week I took a day off and spent it with her, so she could have some special time with me, because she was telling me with her behavior, that she needed it.

While an older sibling is still very much loved, fed and dressed, they still want to feel like the baby. They don't want to be forgotten. It takes a bit of practice to figure out what to address first, a crying baby in the crib or a toddler's needs. Is the baby just fussing itself down for a nap? Or is there a danger? Can the toddler help figure things out or go get a clean diaper for the sibling? What if the older child starts to regress into baby talk and peeing in their pants? Set those limits, "I can't understand baby talk, you are not a baby." As well as, "you'll have to wear a diaper again if you don't use the potty," You can remind them they are not a baby, and also give them time to cuddle, like a baby. As for how to toilet train, don't rush this. There is lots of information out there on how to do it, so I am not going to give instruction here. Just let your child tell you when he or she is ready. And remember talking? You can still talk to your baby or your older child and both can be included in a conversation. I used to jokingly ask my toddler to translate the baby gibberish by telling me a story she thought her baby sister was telling. Your creativity can really make for a fun afternoon even when you might be fantasizing about getting a pedicure or running off to a beach vacation alone. A mother I know with seven kids said, and I am paraphrasing, "it's about the same as having two, only you realize how much longer you'll be a parent when you have this many." Two plus kids is hard, but it is short lived and you'll miss it when it's over.

Electronics and Play

The more you interact with your child or children face to face, the better. I have seen far too many instances where a parent hands a phone or tablet to a young child, again to keep them quiet or behaving, in public. Walking down the street with the child in a stroller, in the car, at the grocery store. I want to stress to you that this is not going to lead to better behavior in the future. Screen time needs to be limited far more than it appears to be. I don't have research to quote on this, but most of us grew up having to look up and see where we are going, ask questions about the world, watch life go by in the car and count how many license plates from other States we can find, and lived to tell the tale. These are glorious moments of life and love with children that too many are missing because of a screen in the face. A young child can help at the store, can enjoy scenery – or simply sing along to the radio, and be bored sometimes to develop an inner life. They have toys to play with and love it when you sit down and show them how to play with a toy or let them guide you. Constant electronic input is going to lead to worse behavior when you have to take it away. We see older kids and their gaming, and toddlers when the screen goes blank – have complete meltdowns when they are told to turn off their electronics. So if you have small kids and you are reading this, don't start. If you have started, work on limiting their use now.

When I had my first child, I had an early model "cellular" phone, as well as a computer for surfing the internet and sending email with photos attached. This wasn't very long ago, but since then, technology advanced and adults have gotten pretty attached to their screens as well. I can't have a discussion about limiting your child's screen time if I don't tell you that the same is true for you. As an old timer, I tend to walk down the street looking where I am going, and my phone is either in a purse or a pocket. I can tell you that what I see is concerning. People are looking down at their phones *everywhere*. They are on the phone in the car, crossing the street, sitting down at a restaurant, waiting for their morning coffee, and yes, while they are with their children – pushing the stroller or at the playground, and not paying attention. I realize you could be reading this book on your phone right now, please be sure to do it when you are not responsible for your child's safety and well-being, like at the swimming pool. When your child sees you constantly looking at your phone, and you try to tell them to limit their use? How well do you think that is going to go over? Put it down, and connect to your children instead.

Misbehavior has a Goal

One of the main parenting instruction books I use and taught is called Systematic Training for Effective Parenting, or STEP by Drs. Don Dinkmeyer and Gary McKay. I read and taught classes in this style before I had my own children and it resonated with me as being quite logical, fair and focused on relationship, not rules and punishment. One of the main ways we can handle power seeking behaviors – because let's face it, toddlers are always seeking more power – is to offer a choice.

Power does not mean they think they can run the world. No, they only want more say over their lives, and when we start small and give them opportunities to make decisions, they grow up feeling like they can make good choices because they have had practice.

STEP talks about the goals of misbehavior – power seeking, attention, revenge and displays of inadequacy (pretending to be helpless or unable). Toddlers generally want either power or attention. The ways in which children make efforts to gain these things will vary with their age. When we think about kids having goals by misbehaving, we realize that it is another way they are trying to communicate. Listening to our own feelings is the best way to identify the goal. If you are angry, the child is seeking power.

Now I don't mean place them in front of the all you can eat buffet of choices all day long. You can't overwhelm them with options, especially when they are young. You'll go from tantruming to full on Godzilla-attacking-Tokyo angry. If you need to get out of the house by a certain time, and your toddler wants to try on and change every pair of pants they own, offer a choice: "you can wear your blue pants or your green pants today," to narrow it down. If the child does not make a choice, you make the choice for them and tell him or her that you can try again tomorrow because now you will be late. Use a firm voice, slowed down words and eye contact to make your point. Do not ask "okay?" when you are done. I hear this constantly after a request or statement from a parent as if they are offering another choice or you are asking for their permission. You are in charge, you can own that and be a loving parent.

I am frequently told by mothers that children respond better to the fathers. They are sure the fathers are scarier than the mothers, and often they think this is the "right way" to parent but they cannot seem to get better cooperation even when they yell and get mad. So here is what I think: fathers do not offer choices when no choice is available. They do tend to have a more stern voice, and they do not give any impression that the child needs to give permission (as in asking "okay?" after a direct instruction). It is simply a matter of style and mothers can still be warm, cuddly givers and also be firm when necessary without the child being afraid and without resorting to spanking. Women are just socialized to be less assertive than men, generally speaking. Men are also, generally, out of the home more, and therefore are slightly more mysterious to toddlers. We tend to see similar results for the parent who is out of the home the most regardless of gender.

A choice is also not an ultimatum. You have to offer two to three reasonable options for them to choose. If you say, "put on your pants or else we won't have dessert tonight," you're not going to get the results you want. First off, as STEP stresses, discipline needs to make sense. What does dessert have to do with getting dressed? The more the child can connect their behavior to an outcome the better they learn. For example, "if you put on your pants now, we will have time to stop and get that ice cream for after dinner, but if we are late, we cannot." Or simply, "if you don't wear the snow pants you will not be able to play in the snow with your friends."

We don't always have to hold a punishment over our kids' heads to get them to behave well. They don't have to be afraid of us to be cooperative. They really do want nothing more than to be with us and be happy. It's easy, again, to parent on auto pilot and just make a threat or get mad and escalate the situation. There is no reason to take a moment and think about what needs to be done when you're in conflict. We, as parents, will need less and less "discipline" if we are more and more tuned into what our child is doing and how we are responding. I continually see blog posts on various popular parenting sites about how "no-one told me" how hard it is going to be. Well, I am telling you here and now. You are going to struggle to do what is right, you are going to fail sometimes. You are going to be exhausted, feel resentful and angry, not recognize yourself, feel guilty and ashamed of your emotions being out of control. You're going to yell and feel like a toddler yourself at times. And, you are going to survive it.

Sometimes we find that we yell a lot at our kids – and believe me I know you don't like it as much if not more as your kids. One of the things I tried when my kids were little was the exercise of pretending I was on TV. In my case, I wanted to be the "expert" who was making a television show on "how to…" How to put your kids to bed, how to get your kids ready in the morning. Imagining that there was a camera on me made me very mindful of my own behavior. I used to watch "Nanny 911" and couldn't believe that parents would not be on their "best" behavior to be on a television show. But, that's about being entertaining. I usually agreed with the nanny when she would review the footage.

Little ones don't necessarily need to be disciplined/punished, but they do misbehave. They are exploring and testing limits, yes. And they need those limits to be set by adults to keep them safe and their environment predictable. It's not about controlling them, as I have read about modern parenting, it's about boundaries, which everyone needs. Common sense prevention is always best – like putting the household chemicals in a top kitchen cabinet instead of below the sink; Putting soft items like dishtowels and napkins in lower drawers and the knives above the counter. You get the idea, right? But when they misbehave, from what you can tell they are really testing those limits by climbing up on a chair to see what they can't have, repeating a curse word they heard – and often in the right context. We need to let them know that they are out of bounds.

Just like in narrating their play, we simply identify their behavior, "You are climbing up onto the counter, it's not safe for you, stay on the floor." Remind them that the adults don't climb up onto the counter (I know sometimes you have to but try to do it when they're asleep), and refrain from using curse words.

I once worked with a toddler who was in a family placement due to abuse and neglect, and when she was done with me, she would look at me and say, "Fuck off," and sometimes "Shut up," which was a surprise! I turned my head holding in my laughter, looked at her caregiver and asked if that was what I heard. Her caregiver said, yes, and responded firmly and angrily to the child that she was "saying bad words." Well, yes, and in the past this little one's cursing was probably a source of entertainment, or she was told to *fuck off* when adults didn't want her around. I didn't know exactly how she learned it because she wasn't able to tell us her life's story. Setting a limit was only one response. I suggested that we give her other words. We want kids to be able to also set limits with peers who are getting into their personal space or taking their toys. I said to the child, "how about, 'leave me alone'?" We continued to give her this alternative language until it clicked, rather than just getting mad and scolding. Kids aren't born knowing what to say or do, we as the parents, have to teach them.

Similarly, I notice a lot of stressed out parents with toddlers in restaurants. Kids have very short attention spans for waiting. Keeping them entertained is hard; especially when the adults are trying to catch up on their lives together, or thinking this is a good time to update their Facebook status. Put away the phone, treat this like a date with someone special. Bring a small toy, move the silverware out of their reach (and anything else), gently remind them to sit in their seat and not climb over booths into the laps of other diners. If they spit out their drink, remove the drink and *tell them*, "You can have it back when you are ready to drink without spitting." They'll get it over time, they really will. Engage your kids in a discussion, help them pick their food off the menu and encourage them to order it for themselves. This age range is not a reason to stay away from all public outings. They need those experiences and interactions. To hell with what the other diners are thinking about you – chances are you aren't taking them to the Four Seasons anyway.

Often, we find ourselves responding to something that isn't even about our child. We had a bad day at work, or we are angry with our partner, or angry for being single, or broke and the child is outgrowing his or her last outfit. We are also unconsciously or consciously responding to our history as a child and memories of our own parents. We make mistakes all the time, but you know what? It's okay to tell your mini-me that you messed up. "I made a mistake," is very powerful to say to a child and for a child to be able to say. Then, we can ask them to forgive us. Yes, we can ask a child for forgiveness. It is humbling, to be sure. It's a part of life, after all. I'm not perfect are you?

We all deserve to get another try another time. As in the earlier story of the young mother with her mother, we are reacting to stress and it is being channeled toward our child. You are not the only one. Talk about these things with other parents, they are going through very similar feelings and most caregivers really want adult conversation and validation. You don't have to have any real answers, just a listening ear and a supportive reply of, "yep, that sounds about right." You may be young, old, rich, poor, black, white, parent or non-parent, but you can look someone in the eye and say, "You are a good parent/mother/father. You may not know everything, but you are doing your best." That someone you tell can even be you. In the mirror. Try it.

Summary

1. Knowing milestones and child development can prevent child abuse.
2. Toddlers are learning to assert their independence but still need guidance and limits.
3. Toddlers need human interaction and stimulation to learn and grow so put the phones and tablets away.

Now You:

1. List 5 positive personality traits your toddler appears to have right now. Who do they seem most like in your family?
2. What activities to you enjoy the most as a parent with your toddler? Why?
3. Do you have any concerns about your toddler's development? Keep a journal of milestones and questions and bring it to the regular check-up appointments.
4. What self-care activities are you doing as a parent? Make a plan to do one thing for an hour just for you once per week.
5. Try the TV show exercise. What did you notice about your parenting?

Play is often talked about as if it were a relief from serious learning. But for children play is serious learning. Play is really the work of childhood.

-Fred Rogers

Chapter 4

Childhood

As promised, your child grows up into a kid who needs to go to school. Kids get bored being home and with parents and sitters all the time. They want to learn, they want to spend time with other kids and make friends. And you, my dear parent, need them to go as well. This is a glorious day and tears may be shed. An interesting tidbit to know – changing schools often leads to worse outcomes for kids. School mobility leads to poorer grades, less engagement and higher drop out rates, according to Education Week Magazine. Make every effort to minimize school changes. Children really need the consistency that school provides. Of course, if you move away, a child promotes or there is some other reason for the change that is out of your control, don't sweat it too much, these have fewer side effects on kids.

Childhood is the realm of birthday parties, emerging talents, best friends, worries and anxiety, and a little or a whole lot of attitude. We learn as parents to let them go more and more – to school, to a play date at a friend's house, or even their first sleep over. We begin to see them show an interest in a few specialized things, like dancing or singing, sports, or science. They are philosophers, recording devices, chatterboxes, worry-warts, and endless sources of energy. Just because the baby stage is over, it doesn't mean all that snuggling and attention has to end, either. The difficult stuff is still there, it is just different difficult stuff.

My older child began a half day preschool program when she was three – she could not wait to go to school and learn. The school asked parents to wait in the teachers break room and check in after an hour or so. Some kids were crying and sad, my child looked at me with the evil eye and told me to go away. Right, errands it is! I wasn't completely free at that point because I had a newborn baby girl with me, but it gave me time to focus on her for a change.

Of course early preschool costs money, we were able to find a program in a local school for kids with special needs that needed "regular" kids to join a class for other kids who were going to transition into regular education programs. So my kid got preschool and the other half of the class got integration services. In other parts of New York City, finding a preschool that didn't cost the same as college was nearly impossible and there is a lot of discrimination out there about either putting your child in with the special education kids, or mixing private pay kids with subsidized/low income kids. It comes from the parents and the programs and it may take a little soul searching on your part to determine what you think really matters to you. Obviously, adequate child care and universal pre-K services are an issue in the US, perhaps not as much in other countries. Kids do need this, so if you can do it, make it happen.

In this chapter we are going to introduce the following skills for children who are misbehaving:

1. Name the behavior specifically and how you know it is happening (you see it with your eyes, hear it with your ears).
2. Tell the child how it makes you (or the other person) feel.
3. Prohibit the behavior and add a consequence if needed.
4. Monitor for more behaviors.

I will go over situations where this can be used, it will repeat throughout the chapters with each age / developmental group.

Let's recap the main concepts we are working with around parenting: respect, communication, empathy, accountability, and relationship. This is the stage where these really kick in and kick our asses. Children realize by this time that we, their parents, are not Gods and Goddesses on high with light and halos over our heads. We make mistakes, say curse words, get into car accidents or get injured, catch the flu, and sometimes do the wrong thing when parenting. Kids also learn that all the scary things in life are real by the time they are five. Five is marked as the final phase of separation anxiety and just in time for them to start kindergarten, isn't that wonderful timing? Many parents have asked me, and I have experienced it first hand, why their five year old is suddenly terrified of everything and won't allow a parent to go out of sight.

This is why: They have figured out that people die, fires burn, lightning strikes, animals bite, and strangers can be scary (Otherwise why would we tell them not to talk to them?) and take them away from their parents. Anxiety, again, comes on when we fear we cannot control everything. This is a good time to demonstrate to your kids that fear is normal, that we are protecting them to the best of our ability, not putting too much responsibility on them before they are ready, and to learn to control the things within their control, shrug off the rest.

A huge skill to teach them now, even in the toddler years, is to take a deep breath. A fun way to learn is to try to blow a big bubble. You take a big breath and very slowly blow into the ring to make a large bubble. When you prompt them to first take a big breath before starting to talk, they are associating that rush of oxygen and relaxation with expressing feelings, so they can talk about hard things while feeling physically calm. Kids can also meditate for short periods of time. By learning to be calm when nothing in particular is going on, that sense of relaxation can follow them when things are stressful. They know how to regulate their breath, clear their minds and focus. Remember how babies regulate? They learn it from mirroring our bodies and feelings.

We show respect to our children when we do not poo-poo their worries. We can listen to them, teach them to take deep breaths, talk about their worries, and reassure them. They're going to drive you mad from time to time with their freak outs about just about everything, but the less you react with high emotion like, "oh for the love of- would you stop it already?" and the more you say (after many of your own deep breaths), "this is really on your mind a lot, huh? What can I help you with?" they will feel less and less out of control and more confident that you are going to take care of things and keep them safe.

Children learn to trust you and rely on you. Encouraging them to openly talk about or express their feelings (i.e. communication) will reduce behavior that is attempting to show emotion instead. When you listen, they feel important to you. Please don't jump ahead in your mind that you are creating a wimpy, wishy-washy, thumb-sucking crybaby. You are actually doing the opposite. When you send them into the world feeling confident and supported, they will carry these secure feelings with them wherever they go.

Communication

Good communication skills matter no matter where you go or how old you are. If your child grows up in a home where people talk about problems, listen to one another, don't jump to conclusions or interrupt, ask questions, make eye contact, show interest in one another, they already have a jump start on life. The good news is, no money is required to do this. You can sit down together at the dinner or breakfast table and talk about each other's day. Couples can work out simple problems in front of the kids to model problem solving and relationship. You can tell funny stories about your own childhood or make plans for the follow night's dinner. It may sound very *Leave It To Beaver-esque*, but it doesn't have to be the Baby Boomer kind of dinner where mom is always getting up to serve someone something or clean up and getting no chance to join in.

I'm not going to dictate what you all discuss from this point – your family is different from anyone else's. Talk about sports, the weather, politics, art, ideas, television shows, as long as you talk and show interest in one another. "Be quiet and finish your dinner," should never be heard at the table. What is the point of having a family, otherwise, if you don't get to know them? When you are old, you're going to need your kids to look after you.

One of the most basic statements in communication goes as follows:

I feel (emotion) when you (behavior) because (reason). For example: I feel *upset* when you *cover your ears as I talk* because *what I am telling you is important*.

When you begin a statement with "you make me," or "you are," all you are doing is shutting down listening. While I would never say you are responsible for someone's feelings, when we talk to children, we need to alter our approach instead of expecting them to change to accommodate our needs. This works on adults as well:

I feel frustrated when you leave the toilet seat up at night because I keep falling in the water. Saying "you need to listen" or "you make me so mad," puts others on the defensive. Starting with how something makes you feel owns your part in it and teaches children that their behavior has consequences for others. I want to caution parents from using the words "appropriate" and "inappropriate" without any qualifiers. It is incredibly vague, leaves so much up to the imagination for kids and way too much wiggle room. Who is to say what is appropriate and when? Are kids now required to read minds? No, always be specific as to why you are setting a limit or initiating a consequence.

Empathy

Empathy is another critical skill for people to develop. It not only helps us tune into our emotions through our bodies and senses, it helps us imagine what others might be feeling. There have been some criticisms that children of a recent generation were given "too much" instruction on empathy. We are just all just social experiments in our respective generations, and the pendulum will swing. Whoever thought of moderation being the best approach was probably a genius. Extremes are always just that – extreme. When we ask our children how it might feel to be the "other kid," the one who is being teased, the one who doesn't like to speak up, the one who looks different from most of the other kids. It is for a reason. We want our kids to be aware of not only how their emotions affect themselves, but stretch their minds to imagine being someone else. "How would you feel if…" We can get to that point, where a child can articulate something so abstract by helping them tune in and recognize their own feelings.

> When your child does something that makes them happy: "you're smile is ear to ear, you must feel so proud right now!"

> When your child seems quiet and sad: "I'm wondering what you're thinking about because you seem a little sad."

> When your child is angry and short tempered: "tell me what is going on, you are angry about something and I want to help you."

There are hundreds of words to describe feelings, and it does help to learn a few more than the basics of happy, sad, mad and afraid. I am providing a list at the back of this book.

Your child may not want to talk, sometimes they decide to rely on their behavior instead. This will piss you off, I am sure. Don't take the bait! You can set limits on the behavior, instead of reacting as a pissed off parent: "it is not okay to act out when you are mad. Go sit on the couch/steps/wherever, and when you are calm and ready, I am here to listen." I wrote "act out" to keep it general. However, anytime you can specifically name the behavior – yell, hit, break things – the better. It keeps things less vague. You may have a child who denies doing anything, "I'm not!" Then be even more specific, "I saw you three seconds ago hit the wall with your shoe. Go sit down and take five deep breaths right now." If they will not, take them by the hand a show them how to take five deep breaths, together. This, as all of the other concepts, can lead to a closer relationship, shows that you are the leader between you, that if they feel out of control, you are still in control of yourself. You are setting the stage for them to safely bring up whatever it was that happened in their day that lead to these intense feelings, and what to do about them. If this was your day at any point, there will be more and you can do it differently the next time. Have some compassion for yourself, this shit is hard.

Couples

You know what else is hard? Parenting with a second person adding to the mix. Yes, I am talking about the people we chose to spend our lives and procreate with or otherwise raise a family with. Our darling, can *do no wrong* spouses, partners, co-parents, or whatever your call them these days. Just if you call them "jerk-face" or "asshole," those sweet terms of endearment need to be kept out of your child's earshot. Seems pretty basic, right? But you might be surprised. How we interact with our children's other parent matters a great big deal. It forms a child's mental image of how relationships are meant to be from a very early age. If you are seeing some concerning behaviors from your child when interacting with friends, family, authority figures, it might be a good idea to take a look at your own interpersonal behavior. They are learning it from somewhere and chances are, it is from you. This matters whether you live with your co-parent or not. If you are still together, get on the same parenting page, now.

As I stated above, my favorite is the STEP program, but you can decide what works best for you. I was fortunate that my ex-husband also taught the STEP program where we used to work. We had the skills already down pat before we ever got together and made pretty babies. As long as you are on the same wavelength with your style and methods, it will make the difference. Earlier I talked about demonstrating basic problem solving at the dinner table, or in the car, etc. However, larger problems that are not for children's ears need to be kept private. Anything that could get heated, or involves a conflict over how one or the other handled a parenting issue should be discussed away from the kitchen table. If something was done that the other parent believed was way out of bounds, the parents can decide how to and if it should be remedied. The child should not get the impression that one parent holds more authority than the other.

I know this is not going to go over well with the more traditional families where the dad has the final word no matter what. But imagine being a dad, coming home and having to make all of the decisions? That seems like it would add a lot more stress than necessary. Parenting is a team effort; it really has to be. When one parent is undermined or overruled constantly, or even occasionally, it sets up a dynamic in the home that will only create conflict going forward. If you are looking around and seeing chaos at home, you know what I am talking about.

Many families also have grandparents or other extended family living in the home. The answer to this dilemma is similar: Parents need to discuss how they will be parenting with the grandparents. If spanking is not acceptable, grandparents will need to know this specifically and adhere to that rule. Discussions of parenting questions need to be held away from the child. The child may be in trouble, but they can wait for the adults to decide what to do. There aren't many instances where justice cannot wait, as long as any danger is over. Your kids are sponges, they are learning at every turn and they will gain such important life skills. Often we think of parenting as what we do to keep the "little brats" alive until they leave home and go out into the world. We forget sometimes, that the daily moments of life in a family teaches them probably more than half (no I don't have a statistic for this) of what they need to know to be successful human beings.

Siblings

If the average family in the United States has two-point-whatever children, there is a good chance you and your child will grow up with a sibling. I had two, one older and one younger, and I am parenting two children today. In an informal survey of my friends on Facebook, about half said they made a point to help their kids get along, and the other half was more hands off, all with differing results. All I really know about siblings is that they are built-in playmates on good days, and your worst enemies on bad days. Why is that? Part of it is because these are the people who know us the best in the world, they know where all of your buttons are and they are willing to push them. They share the same parents and when you grow up you will share a history. If they were there, they will remember. They also might throw it back in your face whenever they can, but they also remember, and have different memories and experiences than you. Most parents want their children to have siblings to have that playmate and have someone who will be in their life until old age. But do most parents even consider how they are going to facilitate a good relationship?

I've seen a lot of creative solutions to petty bickering such as the "get along shirt" where kids have to wear one large shirt and do everything cooperatively in that shirt. With multiple siblings it may be more like a corporate team building event similar to capture the flag. Many daily family activities, vacations and meals seem to work for creating family harmony, when there are emotionally healthy parents with a good blueprint for family life.

I have noticed that while my daughters may come crying to me some days that their sister, "Is being *such a bitch!*" there are times when if I listen, I will hear them giggling and talking in one of the other rooms, which is all I ever hoped for. Some time ago, I added a hand-out to my website to help parents decrease sibling rivalry; I think it is useful to put here:

1. Improve communication. Encourage children to talk about what they are experiencing when they

are engaging in overly argumentative behaviors/rivalries with sibling

2. Improve Empathy. Encourage children to imagine he/she is being treated the way they are treating the sibling. What would it feel like to be in their shoes? Help the child find words for emotions they are feeling.

3. Accountability or Consequences. The children will be given a consequence that makes sense. They must choose a "chore" from the jar (see below), or do something kind for the sibling.

Common Emotions:

Irritated, annoyed, frustrated, hurt, unimportant, sad, angry, lonely, jealous, tired, ignored.

Experiencing these feelings can trigger an outburst. Parents can identify these and interrupt the child's cycle by doing the above interventions before the child reacts. Our Encourage cooperation and healthy competition through games and play, do not allow name calling, hitting (even lightly), or cheating. Give them chores to complete together for a mutual benefit (if we finish by 1 we can go to the movies, play a game, go to park).

CHORE JAR
create jobs on slips of paper and put into a container. When a child behaves abusively toward the sibling,

he/she must choose a slip of paper and complete the task immediately.

- Sweep porch
- Sweep floor or run vacuum cleaner on first floor/second etc.
- Wipe counters and lower kitchen cabinets (depending on height of child)
- Load and/or Empty dishwasher
- Neaten up family room (bring personal items to room, straighten pillows, take cups to kitchen etc.)

- Clean mirrors and glass in house
- Dust surfaces
- Fold laundry
- Wipe baseboards
- Organize pantry closets
- Scrub household toilets

Something Kind: put away their laundry, lay out school clothes for them, serve their next meal to them, bring them a cup of juice, write them a kind note of what they appreciate about the sibling.

Siblings truly are our first best friends and confidants. As I get older, I am finding out more and more about the inner lives of my siblings, and how living in the same home can in fact lead to completely different experiences. These conversations can lead to even as closer understanding of your own childhood as well as answer questions about things that might have seemed weird growing up, or resulted in strain as adults. This seems to come from the different messages each child got growing up about abilities and personality.

Parents can do incredible harm through comparison, favoritism, leaving the older one in charge all the time, as some examples. Even simple nicknames, assigning a "title" to a childlike "the talented one," or "the athlete," or a pattern of teasing can drive a wedge between siblings by creating categories where there is no overlap allowed. All kids are different, even the identical twins. They can have vastly different temperaments, talents, interests, or the same ones. Their styles may be very different, but both having merit. You, as a parent, can love all of them and all of what they bring all at the same time. Be open to what reveals itself.

You will see that I say this a lot in the later chapters – watch your mouth, what you expect is powerful. The values of using communication, empathy and accountability can easily be incorporated into the sibling relationship, and as you continue reading you will find more helpful uses. The chore list is also a handy tool for managing the household in general – double win! If you are struggling, keep reading, much of the information in this book can be applied to the sibling relationship.

Culture

In the year that I am writing this, I am finding myself shocked at how many people, who once may not have openly talked about their prejudices, are literally wearing t-shirts promoting "white supremacy." I put that term in quotes because I consider that phrase a work of fiction. As in, it is not true, a completely made up concept. Asylum seekers from Central America coming to the Southern US border are being detained in concentration camps as we speak, notice no quotes there. What on Earth is going on? Most of us live in cities, suburbs and towns that are made up of many cultures, skin colors, national origins, religions and languages. Where I grew up, in New York City, I didn't know there were neighborhoods that were not mixed until I was almost an adult. How boring, I thought, to live someplace where everyone looked the same.

As parents, we teach our kids not only social skills, but social norms. And those norms might look different depending on what your parents taught you, and how diverse your community was. I am speaking from the perspective that you teach your children to be kind, inquisitive and open to learning about other human beings at all times. To not assume any negative intent from someone based on their skin color, to not infer intelligence (or the lack thereof) based on what language they speak, that they speak up for injustice when they see it. You may come from a family where, traditionally, they see other people as inferior to themselves. You don't have to teach your kids the same thing. You can say, "Yes, it is true, grandpa did not say nice things about black people, but what he said about them is *not true*."

You may also need to explore the beliefs you may be holding about other groups of people, your child will follow your lead and learn to self-examine and question what they are being told. The sooner you start this, the sooner your child will.

You may be raising a child who is in a minority group in their area, and you may also have to have some tough conversations. There will be some people who treat them differently, and badly in some cases. Your child may have to learn some scary things to survive, like how not to be targeted by security when shopping in a store, if at all possible. These will be hard discussions and their first experiences of discrimination will be heartbreaking. This is another topic that could cover an entire other book, but I want to plant a seed in your mind that this could be an ongoing topic with your family, and I hope that it is no matter where you are from.

Mental Health

I see a lot of posts, memes, blogs about parenting, about how our kids "drive us crazy" or got into trouble at school for some mischief or even for bullying another child. I have friends ask me often if they should take their child to counseling for sometimes "normal" things related to the child's particular temperament, and sometimes for what is a good catch on the part of the parent. How would you know if your child is having issues beyond what you, as a parent, can help?

The critical question I am going to ask is, "does the child's behavior or mood prevail across two or more environments?" If a child is struggling to concentrate in school, misbehaves, can't stay in their seat and blurts out in class, but is quiet and pleasant at home, sits and reads, then I would think there is some school anxiety vs ADHD (attention deficit hyperactivity disorder). If a child is moving and off task at home and at school, and in a museum and a grocery store, then we might be looking at ADHD. Confused already? That's why getting answers from a person and not your Google search is important. There is a lot to consider and asking is perfectly reasonable. Children with ADHD don't always need a therapist, unless some of their adaptive behaviors have become habits and they need help with social skills and parents may need help adapting their own skills to the child who needs a lot of patience. Kids can usually be easily treated with medication that the pediatrician can prescribe (a simple questionnaire should be given to the teacher and an EKG is usually completed first). Be sure to ask a lot of questions – parents need to know everything they can.

Similarly, the concerning behavior is not only taking place in multiple environments, it is also interfering with normal daily tasks. A child who is developing OCD (obsessive-compulsive disorder) will eventually forego pleasurable activities to complete the compulsive behavior they "need" to complete to resolve the worry in their mind. Most people have a superstition or two, but if a child cannot get dressed before going through several perfect renditions of their task, (flipping the light switch, a chant, touching objects in a certain order) there is a problem.

If you have answered "yes" to either or both of the above questions (2+ environments, interfering with fun), you may need a professional consultation. It does not mean something is "wrong" with your child, or your parenting. Imagine if your child needed a life-saving medical service, and you decided, "no, it'll be okay without the intervention." You wouldn't likely do that, would you? You'd take your child for the appointments until they were cured. Letting an emerging mental illness go untreated is a threat to the child's future, so it's better to get help now while their brains are workable. Yes, many of these illnesses also come out as adults, and we can't always predict it, but kids can learn valuable coping skills to handle stress throughout their lives. And parents don't always know the best way to manage childhood anxiety, depression, OCD, ADHD. When you love someone as much as you love your child, your emotions get mixed in all too easily.

Ask your child if they are worried about anything. Tell them you can find someone who can help them feel better. It might not even take very long for relief. A good child therapist can help bring out issues through drawing, through games and help the child identify and verbalize what is worrying them. The therapist can help parents respond more effectively to their child and teach them skills to self-regulate, communicate and listen. Call a therapist, ask the questions, and make the appointment. A wonderful adulthood awaits your child.

Keeping Your Children Safe

When your child is being groomed, the parents are as well, especially when it is someone you know. What do I mean by "grooming?" The person who wants to have access to your child wants to gain your trust, and often they are in a position of trust. When they begin to test that trust, you begin to question yourself, "now why would they want to take Suzie out but not Sally?" They will make you think you are crazy and a terrible person for ever questioning their motivation.

In a nutshell there are 6 stages of grooming, the following are the most agreed upon:

1. Targeting the victim. The perpetrator will observe and decide who would make the best victim. It may be the child who wants and enjoys attention and struggles with friendships.

2. Gaining the victim's trust. This adult most likely has said, *you are growing up now, you can make decisions for yourself. You don't always have to ask or tell your parents everything.*

3. Filling a need. I can take you places you can't go on your own, that your parents won't let you.

4. Isolating the victim. I'm your friend, they are not your friends. Only I can do *xyz* for you.

5. Sexualizing the relationship. The perpetrator will initiate sexual contact.

6. Maintaining control. Keeping the victim from disclosing, using threats, gifts and other forms of coercion.

If you find out something like this is going on, stay calm. Most parents' first instinct is probably more raw - we want to lay down the law right off the bat. "You better not ever see that guy or write to that guy again," with a lot of cursing perhaps thrown in. The thing is, that reaction could harm the parental relationship. A school aged child might not understand the sudden cutting off of contact and ask questions. A teen will likely push back even harder. "He said you were going to do/say that!" and then you have more secrecy to be concerned about. It is best to approach it within the context of your close and loving relationship. Spend some time building on that with some quality time and attention. Follow up on the information, make a report to the police if there is more to the story, and then keep your eyes peeled and your ears to the ground.

Keeping your eyes on your child when you are out of the home or have visitors, and knowing their whereabouts you will keep them safe. Asking a child to protect themselves from predators is a common misconception, i.e. "run away from as stranger, yell, fight." Adult or even teen predators are stronger and smarter than your child and your supervision is the most effective way to prevent harm from coming to them. Take a deep breath.

High Risk Behavior and Accountability

Getting back to the list of parenting values – the one I consider the hardest is accountability. This is not just punishment or discipline. This is about teaching a child to take ownership of mistakes at a much deeper level, so that they do not grow up into someone who holds themselves to a standard above anyone else. When we allow children and adults to get away with anything from an annoying daily infraction to abusive behaviors against others, the behavior will only get worse. We know this because we see it all the time, most often in the news, especially when someone commits a serious crime and there is no consequence for it.

One of the trainings I do regularly is called "Preventing Primary Perpetration," and goes all the way up to parenting and managing adolescents who have engaged in some pretty serious abuse of others including sexual assault. This curriculum was developed by a team of behavioral experts and professionals at the Kempe Center in Denver, Colorado over 25 years ago, and I have found it useful in managing all kinds of behaviors in kids and adults. So sit back and get ready for some meat and potatoes, you are not likely to find this in other parenting books for the general public. Everyone has a cycle: it can be pretty mild or it can lead us to high risk behaviors. But we all do it. First, someone or something "triggers" us.

My favorite example is being cut off in traffic. It pisses most of us off – no one has time to get into an accident, and how dare that jerk for cutting into our path when we need to get someplace important? Please refer to the graphic below. Think of a clock – the old fashioned kind.

Your trigger is at 12:00. As the minute hand move down to

1:00, you're feeling sorry for yourself, "aw man, now I am gonna be late" or even lose your job and you're feeling pretty sorry for yourself. However, you start

THE HIGH RISK CYCLE

thinking that Karma needs to get that shit head for cutting you off, and that maybe Karma is your middle name. You imagine slipping ahead of that car and cutting him off! Yeah, that'll teach him, he'll be sorry he ever cut you off. Now most of us do enjoy a good fantasy of sweet revenge, and most of us leave it as a fantasy. We have that little voice in us that tells us to stop being stupid and let it go. Or we should… When we are young, we don't always have that little voice fully developed. As parents,

we have to help kids develop their own conscience by being their conscience for a while. A trigger isn't usually a particular event that sets the cycle into motion: it is a feeling that comes up for us. Feeling shut down by someone, feeling left out, feeling unappreciated, feeling let down, feeling overly criticized. These are often unconscious and immediate and kids as well as adults don't always realize it has happened. A parent's empathy for their own child is going to help tune in to these.

We need to notice when our children appear upset. When they go off and isolate, they may be plotting their fantasy and revenge. This is a good time to go find them, hear them out, help them find new ways of coping with their feelings, with the event that triggered the feelings. Help them tap into their strengths. Get them involved in a pro-social activity like a game or helping with a chore.

The trick is when they've done the deed. Most bad behaviors have a goal as well as a triggering event or thought. As STEP has told us for years, kids want Power, Attention, Revenge and to Display Inadequacy (to get out of doing something) when they misbehave. An abusive behavior can get them all four of these things. What do I mean by "abusive behavior?" Keeping in mind that we are in my Childhood chapter, let's think of some of the fun things kids do to drive parents crazy. Kids will: write on the walls, tear up a sibling's toy, throw something fragile on the ground, spit, yell mean things or curse, run off and hide, steal, hurt a pet, or hurt another child. Abuse can be toward property, another person or themselves.

When a child has completed a behavior, they need to be held accountable. On the clock, above, we see that at the 11:00 mark, the child will deny doing the behavior. Keep in mind that this does not represent 24 hours, this cycle can go in minutes and in rapid succession with several behaviors. What if we, the parents, don't even see the child doing the deed and we don't want to scapegoat them all the time? The first offense can often mean the last offense. This is what is meant by Primary Prevention. We can often stop unwanted behavior before it begins. Paying attention and listening to children play is a pretty good habit, even if that trashy novel and park bench at the playground is calling your name.

> Here is a brief play by play of how we can stop behaviors from getting worse: Jenny: "Hey! Greg, stop, that's mine!" Greg takes Jenny's toy and throws it up in the air repeatedly so she can't get it back. Jenny begins to cry.

Parent: "Greg, Jenny, come here."

Greg: "I didn't do anything!" He throws Jenny's toy at her feet and she picks it up.

Parent: Greg, I saw you with my eyes. You took Jenny's toy away. Jenny is sad that you did that, and it was a bad choice to take it.

This is where it could stop. You, the parent, informed the child, Greg, that he made a bad choice and his behavior made another person feel sad. He may decide to not do that again simply because he was called out for it. So what if he does something again?

Parent: "Greg, I told you before that taking Jenny's toy made her sad and it was a bad choice. I am feeling sad, too, because I know you can do better (acceptance and encouragement). Now you are doing it again (or specifically name the newer behavior). This must stop. Now you have a consequence of sitting on the bench for 5 minutes."

Greg knows what his behavior was and what the consequence is for doing it. He is learning empathy when feelings are being pointed out to him. He is given a chance to make a better choice. If his behavior continues, the consequences can escalate until he loses his time at the park all together. STEP stresses that there are times when a parent does not need to get involved, even in a case like this where we have similar age kids, and no one is being hurt. However, I believe instead that teaching children that adults are paying attention and intervening can be very powerful for them. They need this kind of accountability most of the time and as early as possible well before behaviors escalate.

If you find that your child is constantly or just frequently "getting into trouble," there is a good chance they are in the cycle and going around and around. Where can you intervene? The best intervention point is in the isolation phase, around 4PM. Once you begin to recognize misbehaviors as being a part of a high risk cycle – when the resulting behavior is abusive, you can anticipate issues by identifying triggers and de-escalate a situation before it gets to the "poor me" phase.

At this point I am going to insert the useful phrase "Trigger Warning" to talk about the next topic. You may need to get up and get some water, go to the bathroom, get regulated in other words, but you really can't avoid this: Kids are born with sexual feelings. They are human, after all. They learn about sex and sexual behavior throughout their lives, but the feelings are natural and biological. If you have a boy, you know what I mean, because they get erections all the way back in infancy. Accepting that girls have sexual feelings as well has been more of a challenge for society at large, because we can't usually see it as clearly, and because they are in diapers. When kids reach the age of 3 or so, they develop more find motor skills in their hands, and can happily play with themselves wherever they go, also because they are now usually out of diapers. It's a whole new world for them. So if you happen to notice your five year old humping a pillow while watching cartoons, it is not necessarily because someone abused them. Do not jump to this conclusion. What can you do, then? One of my favorite responses to this was developed by the team at the Kempe Center that I mentioned above.

> "That is private behavior, and this is not a private place."

When you calmly ask your child, "What are you doing there?" and they say something like, "I'm making myself feel good," because, it does feel good. So you reply with, "Yes, it does, but that *is private behavior and this is not a private place*." Simple, to the point, non-shaming, and sets a limit without forbidding it all together. Parents who are very conservative may struggle with not forbidding it outright. But you are usually tucking them in at night and staying until they are asleep or leaving right away. Frankly, what they do behind closed doors is none of your business. We want our children to grow up and have loving relationships with other adults that includes a healthy sex life.

Another popular and likely scenario among children is a little hanky-panky in the playground or a playdate that you are fortunate enough to show up for. Yaaay. Once again, breathe deeply, don't panic, this does not automatically mean anyone has sexually abused your child or someone else's. If you need to get back up and regulate yourself at this point, feel free. Okay, let's continue. If you see two or even three similar aged kids giggling while fondling one another, for example, fear not. They may stop when they see you, or not. You – calmly – say, "Children, I see you touching each other's privates, and it is making me feel uncomfortable." That's it. Just wait right there. Like the first example with Jenny and Greg, you may not need to say another word.

You keep your eyes on the kids, listen for conversations, plans or language that pricks up your ears. If at another time, or day, you see it again, you do this: "Children, I see you again touching each other's privates, and I told you it made me feel uncomfortable. It looks like it makes Jenny (name of one of the kids) feel uncomfortable too. Now you need to stop." We have added that prohibition at this point, because we're not crazy after all. We don't want to encourage this.

When kids are giggling, they are usually feeling playful. We want to pay attention to signs of emotional distress. If your child or someone else's child spontaneously tells you that someone has hurt them in a sexual way, full stop. You do not ask questions, you call the child abuse hotline in your State or County and make a report, or you support another parent in doing it for their child.

Concerning behaviors are also such because they may involve coercion or force. It is important to address any instances of aggression against peers, or if there is a clear imbalance of strength or power among children such as age or ability (i.e. one child has Down Syndrome).

Consent is also something parents need to keep their eyes open for. Does your child understand what they are being asked to do? Are they developmentally capable and if they say no to a proposal will it mean the risk of losing a friendship? Interpersonal high risk behaviors – the ones where kids harm other people, generally trigger the most reaction from adults.

Be aware that abuse can be by someone unrelated, or by a member of the family – a cousin, or a sibling; an adult, adolescent or child. Prevention tends to focus on parents learning to be non-abusive, and forgets that the children who experienced the abuse have learned some terrible lessons and that classic pecking order sits quietly festering, overlooked. If a boy grows up watching his father abuse his mother, should it surprise anyone that the boy grows up to abuse his partners? The past is not prediction, thank goodness. When children have balance between the negative and the positive they stand more of a chance.

If your child tends to be aggressive or wants to play roughly, other children need to be capable of meeting that child's aggression with similar abilities. Your child may need to channel his or her needs into a formal activity where they can learn both self-control and boundaries. If their need for aggression seems anxious or worrisome to you, by all means sit down and ask them about it. It may not be significant but it does wonders for your relationship.

This has been a serious discussion, and it might seem overwhelming. The majority of you aren't going to need to use this information that much, thankfully. I'm including it because I feel that the systems that address children's abusive behaviors haven't made these skills very accessible to the public. We know what to do, we know how to treat kids and teens who abuse others. So why aren't we, the professionals, shouting it from the rooftops when parents are hungry to know this stuff? Why keep it in the small circles? I don't know but I'm done waiting for someone else to do it.

I'm not saying this is easy- um of course not, remember the title of this book? It's emotionally charged, triggering and scary AF. Most of the parents who are attending my seminars on this topic are being compelled because something has already happened. What I'm saying is these issues and problems can be prevented before they ever start. But it would be worse to see your child do something illegal and go to "juvie" for it. Do you know the age of culpability in your state? That is, at what age can they be arrested and prosecuted? It could be anywhere from 9-12 years old. You and your child need to know this, and they need to know what illegal behavior is so they can refrain from doing it. Parents and school staff somehow fail to know this or educate kids about it yet we expect them to know it.

Monitoring

How do we monitor behaviors without being excessive and giving kids opportunities to grow and learn?

OBSERVATION – Noticing patterns of behavior, objectifications or putdowns, coercion, isolation or withdrawal, anger, power struggles, denial or rationalizing, blaming or projecting, "poor me" syndrome, sexualized language or behaviors.

Ex: *I saw you with my own eyes when you pushed your sister.*

Ex: *I heard you say that you hated him and were going to get him later.*

EXPLORATION – Feelings, thinking errors, empathy, triggers to bad feelings or behaviors.

Ex: *Help me understand what that was about. You must have been really angry.*

EDUCATION – Correct sexual misinformation, social skills, assertiveness, communication, laws/illegal information.

Ex: *What could you have said instead? Would an I-message have worked better?*

Ex: *Hurting someone like that has consequences such as being arrested.*

LIMIT SETTING – restricting activities or places to go, type of language allowed.

Ex: *It's not okay to yell and push.*

Ex: *Because of your choice, we can't go to the zoo today like we planned.*

REDIRECTING – finding alternative activities or communication.

Ex: *Instead of wrestling, let's find a board game to play together.*

BEHAVIOR MANAGEMENT – restriction, safety plans, rewards and costs for behaviors.

Ex: *You did all of your chores today! Pick a reward from the list!*

Ex: *Your safety plan (to be discussed in a later chapter) says you must go with a grownup. Otherwise you can't go.*

Be sure to keep a journal of these things over time. Children do improve with time and consistency. Don't give up and get support.

Encouragement

I use the word encouragement in my first example, because it is also a powerful tool in helping to hold kids accountable for their actions. Encouragement may be a long word, but it is a simple concept. We praise our kids when they accomplish something – finish a project, win a race, earn a treat. When we encourage a child, it means we see them. We notice them, we are aware of all of the steps they took to reach a goal. Some examples of encouraging statements:

> You are putting so much effort into learning piano. I hear how much you practice.

> Your doggy really loves it when you brush him.

> Your drawings are getting better every day.

> I love it when you help me get the table ready for dinner.

You've done it before, you'll be great the next time, too.

Here is what it is not – giving a child a compliment, and then taking it back in the same or following sentence. An example I hear most often: "Wow, you got an A, finally," or "You cleaned your room! It took long enough." These sarcastic, back-handed compliments are sowing seeds of resentment in your child. They really do need to hear from you that you think they are awesome. It needs to be genuine and sincerely expressed. They spend too much time every day trying to impress you – from jumping over the line on the sidewalk, to their artwork, to a new hairstyle. You don't have to be "Tiger Mom" all the time and expect perfection; you can give them constructive feedback without crushing their spirit, your words toward them are powerful.

Encouraging statements are free, kids just have to be themselves; they don't have to earn it or do anything special. Just get to know them and let them know that you see them. They'll eat it right up. Consistently showing a child your attention to who they are may even prevent misbehavior. They won't need to act out to get attention. When they get to make choices, they don't seek out power in negative ways. When they feel heard and listened to, they don't need to take revenge and get you back, and when they feel competent, they won't need to act helpless. You will in turn enjoy much more of parenting, have much less instances of being the bad guy and having to punish, ground or lecture.

Constructive feedback is something we'll all get at one point or another in our lives. As I said, it does not need to be cruel or mean-spirited. We have all been told, perhaps by a jealous playmate, that our picture is terrible, or something similar. Maybe that playmate wasn't so important so what they said doesn't matter. But a parent matters. "Mom look at my picture, I want to give it to dad for his birthday!" Perhaps you see something that seems unfinished, or you aren't sure what it is. Ask questions, "what is this about? Did you intend for those two colors to get mixed together? What about this blank area? Does it need something?" Or a simple, "Daddy's going to love your picture." Just giving your attention to their accomplishment will encourage them to make more art and explore their creative side. This is an example for a drawing, but can be used for any kind of creation you are presented with. You are in the moment, not worrying about them becoming a "starving artist" someday. On the other hand, if you are on a conference call or concentrating on something, a child should not be shoving their picture in your face. You can set limits, turn your back holding up a finger to indicate, "wait." When you are done, then you turn around.

The up-front work will make the end of the road much more pleasant. I will talk about managing more serious concerns when I get to the teen chapters, but like I said, implementing the ideas I have already discussed will likely prevent any worse behaviors in the future.

Play

If you read the quote before this chapter by the wonderful Mr. Fred Rogers, you might have expected to see a little bit about play and kids. Fear not, I have it for you here. The concept of play was first discussed by Jean Piaget, a Swiss child developmental psychologist from the early 20th Century. By observing children, mostly his own, he developed many of the theories we use today for child development, although most of us don't know or recall the lingo from school; we just take it for granted now. Kids need time to just play freely. We want our kids in lessons of all sorts, going to museums, going on errands with parents, doing chores. But if we do not give them the space to simply explore their own imagination, either alone or with a friend or sibling, we are not giving them the full childhood experience. I don't mean just a few times a month, this needs to be pretty regular. My mother put herself through school when I was a child, and while she was typing and studying, my sister and I barely moved from our room because we had turned our space into a Barbie doll heaven for the entire weekend. Our Barbies had developed characters, families, jobs, plot lines and relationships. We mimicked situations we had at home, saw in movies or on the news. We made clothing and furniture for them to add to what we had.

When my sister was very sick at the age of seven and had to be hospitalized, we processed out each of our experiences – me not being able to visit her, and her having to go through it – through our Barbie stories. And I loved getting to play with all the new Barbie things she got as gifts during her stay. We wrapped Barbie's legs and arms up in toilet paper and scotch tape to represent a child my sister saw who was "in traction." She told me about the IV that was placed in her hand and how much it hurt, so of course, Barbie had one too. I don't think it is a coincidence that I became a Play Therapist.

When parents play with their children, they often get in the way by introducing rules and concepts that kids don't want. Play is the only time a child has to be in control and in charge of the adults. I beg you parents: let them tell you what to do. Let them give you an assignment. If they want you to play a game you don't like, play it anyway. If they want you to do summersaults, do them. Secondly, help them to laugh. I don't mean tickling them. That is fun in limited amounts, but tickling takes away the child's control and forces laughing. Be silly, do a silly dance or make faces at them. The good feelings that are paired with giggling will be associated with fun times with you and their love will only grow.

Structured time is usually also a part of being a parent. You want your kids to have as many classes and experiences as possible. Pay attention to their talents and interests. Just because you were forced to play violin every waking moment does not mean your child will miraculously inherit some musical gene from you at birth and grow up to be the next Mozart. Our kids cannot fulfil our dreams; demanding that they perform for your approval only fulfils your narcissism and will make your child struggle to become who they were meant to become. If you are struggling with this idea, it may be time to discuss your own anxieties with a therapist.

However, your child often wants to do the things that you do so they can be with you and learn from you. This seems to be the rule although somehow, I got kids who wanted nothing to do with my interests. Oh well. Instead, I followed their leads and they are happy thus far. If you happen to find that your child does have particular talents, do what you can to nurture them. This may involve some sacrifice. Insisting that they can have piano lessons only if the teacher can come to your house on your schedule may not be the exact solution. Your child may need someone really good and that person may require the student to come to them. What is it worth to you? I am not trying to guilt you, but if your expectations are very high, then help your child get there in the best way you can.

Social Lives

Kids this age also want to develop a little more independence from you. Of course they still love you, but they are making friends at school, at gymnastics and baseball practice. They want to go over to other kids' houses and have sleep overs. Many parents are not sure of when children should be doing these things; many parents were kids and may or may not have had bad experiences at other people's homes, or at least have heard of them. This makes us terribly anxious and want to keep our kids wrapped in bubble wrap until they are 21.

First, know your child. If you have a confident and outgoing child who is eager to stay the night with their friend, they probably won't be calling you for a pick up at 2AM. Those nights are miserable for the invitee and the host, so we'd like to avoid it if we can. If your child seems unsure, then wait. Generally, kids are around 7 or 8 when they can manage a sleep over with a non-family member. Second, know the parents. It is perfectly okay to ask to come in at the drop off time, take a look around, ask who lives there, ask who else will be at the house, ask if the alcohol is locked up or if they have guns in the home and are they locked in a safe. This is your child and if you are wondering about these things, so is the host parent when they send their kids out. Third, parents if you can get a night off from time to time, this is a gift. You can pay it back by hosting the other child the next time. You need this break; your kids have fun and you may make a friend in the other parent. It's a win-win.

Summary
1. Your child can learn self-regulation, empathy, communication and accountability
2. Your child will lead the way in terms of their interests, friends, readiness for growth
3. There is help for children who develop mental health concerns

---

Now you:
1. List 5 things you do or could do to encourage your child/children.

2. List 5 things you really like about your child/children.
3. List 5 things that you worry about for your child/children. Why do you think you worry about those things?
4. List 3 things you might do differently after reading this chapter.

You can only be young once. But you can always be immature.

-Dave Barry

Chapter 5

Tweens, Teens and Total Jerks: It's not personal

When I was twelve, I went to Junior High School, and it lasted two years. These days, kids finish Elementary after fifth grade ends and they stay in Middle School for three years. I really don't know why this change happened, it took place sometime while I was away at college and did not give rat's ass about any of that. I assumed the world would just keep spinning the way it always had. But that is the typical immature brain for ya, we think the world we live in will always be the world we live in. We don't see past our front doors until our brains fully develop in adulthood.

Another thing that was added to this stage of development was this word "tween" to describe the period of childhood that falls between childhood and adolescence; but in my experience, adolescence seems to start a bit earlier than most of us expect. For girls, at least, I noticed some serious raging going on starting around age nine. Friends with boys also notice an uptick in strong emotional responses, but boys have hormones as well. Interestingly, this is also the age when "best friends" tend to form in school, so I wonder if it is simply social angst spilling over at home. At ten, kids perfect the eye roll, and get mighty sassy. Anyway, we can't really tell when the "tween" years start so I will stick to the middle school age group – eleven to thirteen. And yes, they are very much in the middle of being kids and being, um, bigger kids. Because let's face it, they are in no way near being young adults just yet. But oh, the hormones.

Have we got hormones! We have attitude, pimples, first periods, involuntary boners, stress eating, crushes and general angst. If you have seen the Netflix series Big Mouth, you will see the most real, raw and honest depiction of the middle school years ever displayed. It occasionally borders on animated child pornography, but it is incredibly spot on. Kids in middle school are struggling with all of these things as well as adults with no boundaries, hormone monsters, social pressures, emerging sexuality and body consciousness. I don't recommend the show, if am to be honest, for kids who are actually in middle school, however.

As odd as it sounds, my middle schooler didn't know much of the information that was being presented until she watched that show. She may have gotten a little bit more of an education that I would have wanted at this time, because the show isn't exactly in an educational format. It's humor, and it's really meant for an older crowd, preferably one that remembers what those young years were like but are past them now. Parents used to have a lot more control over what media their children were able to see. Now we have streaming shows, on demand, no waiting until after 9PM for someone to say "damn" on network TV. And today's kids have it right in the palm of their hands on their little smart phones.

All those early years of taking your child to sports and lessons were also for this good reason: they have something going for themselves other than their Fortnite scores. This builds resilience, time management skills, character, discipline and generally will make them that much more interesting in social situations. Kids who know they have good skills and "a life" also tend to have better self-esteem than kids who are bored. Developmentally, kids are figuring themselves out – who they are or want to be, what they prefer, etc. Having experiences helps them do that – it's a thing to add to their mental list of self-description. Knowing who they are will also protect them from a lot of outside influence and there will be a TON of that.

As I write this, I realize that I'm in the middle of middle school with my second child. The waters are getting murkier for me because I'm less objective than I would be about babies and toddlers. When I start writing about older adolescence I am going to have to separate myself as well. Thankfully, I have other sources to back me up. When it is happening to you, it's hard to stay rational. I'm sure there have been some, "oh sure, easy for you to say," reactions to the earlier chapters. I can say I think I am doing better than a lot of parents, but again, I am more equipped than most parents when it comes to kids.

I fully recall my two middle school/junior high school years as being some of the most trying times of my life, for internal (about me) and external (about the world around me) reasons. For that reason, I have extra empathy for kids this age and they are clearly going through some of the same rights of passage and rigamarole that their parents went through. The majority of calls I get for therapy services are for kids this age, with depression and anxiety.

Mental Health

Just like with the toddler, early teens are stunned by how strong their emotions are. It is a little like going through the toddler stage again and they don't know what to do about the feelings. They can be so intense, kids readily say they want to die to get relief – and we have to take that seriously. We see kids trying smoking/vaping, cutting, numbing out with social media, to calm some of those feelings down. Why cutting? Well, physical pain can be explained more readily to a young mind. It's a distraction and it makes sense though simple cause and effect. Then the emotions kick in about it – all of the negative beliefs about themselves, just like in the cycle in the previous chapter. *I deserve to hurt, I don't deserve love*, are among some I have heard. Something or someone triggers those feelings and they go around the high risk cycle. Abuse is abuse, and kids who harm themselves are experiencing hurt similar to a kid who is being a bully to his or her peers. The causes come from the same place, the behaviors and expressions of hurt are different. The response is not all that different.

Of course, reading this is going to be difficult, you want your kid to be happy and cheery and in love with life, going to dances and the pool, climb on the rocks, swing in the park, ride a rollercoaster and not have a worry in the world. When you are an involved and active parent as early as possible, your kids can be all these things. Many kids don't want to talk to their parents anyway, despite being super cool, open and accepting of them. You can't control that, all you can do is offer your help, and then wait, still being your awesome self. Many parents who have kids who are struggling with any of the above are not to blame, either. Mental illness can strike in any family, but you must be willing to look at yourself and how you can parent differently to address your child's needs, not just pass it off to a therapist to "fix."

As I have said, I see a fair number of adolescents in my practice. I enjoy them a lot because when I was in High School I was in therapy and it damn near saved my life. Not because I was suicidal, but because I was able to process out all of the stupid, silly, stressful and annoying parts of being a teenager and decide what was right for myself. I wanted to go to counseling – I asked to go. It meant my mom spending a little money on me every week but I babysat a lot and I often paid for my own luxuries that way so why not? I could walk to the office on my own, and I was a good client – only missing one or two appointments.

Parents now ask for counseling for their kids – and they should. I always ask if the teenager wants to come, and usually they do. I explain that I am not the snitch for the parents – in front of them both. The kid needs to be able to tell me things without the parent hearing ALL. But the parents also need to be involved to a degree, so they know what progress is taking place and any changes that need to happen so they can support their budding adult.

A therapist cannot "fix" anyone's kid. There are times, when the teens behaviors are direct result/rebellion of their parents' behavior. In those cases, a teen can learn healthy ways to deal with their parents so they can move out someday and lead a healthy life. These are very difficult situations from my point of view. But when it works, the parent sees "improvement" because the teen stops butting heads with the parent as much. The kid sees the end date ahead – graduation, college and eventual independence. Often teens don't realize until you point it out, that they WILL grow up and they CAN live somewhere else. The ability to imagine the future is located in the pre-frontal cortex of the brain, which is not yet fully developed in humans until we become adults. But we can give them a little nudge.

Teens and tweens really get a bad rap about how obnoxious they are – they are so insecure at this age due to the rapid physical changes, how each kid is growing at different rates (some girls have boobs, some don't), who is popular, who is pushed out, feeling pressure to get good grades but also lacking energy and motivation.

No wonder they're moody! Most of the time, they learn to put up a wall to protect themselves, because truly, they don't exactly know who they are inside but when there is this much going on, shutting down or peeking out over the wall of a simpler identity like "Class Clown" or "Popular Girl" seems like the easiest solution. So they act one way with their peers, come home and act another way, and so on. I also see a lot of advice out there about how to deal with these behaviors and most of them talk about accountability, and more of the same parental, authoritarian tone that kids love to push back against. Yes, we do need to hold them accountable, but life can't just be about marching to the beat of the drum and falling in line. As the adults, we need to speak their language a little more, give them plenty of opportunities to grow and make good decisions, and give them space to become who they are meant to be. It's a balance between showing complete unconditional love while letting them know that you are the boss of the house.

Unfortunately, a little "getting over" on parents is part of growing up, and very common. Be patient with your teen. They'll make mistakes and they'll learn from them. It won't usually ruin their whole lives. You can warn them but they'll still insist on finding some things out the "hard way." Listen to them, ask questions, repeat back what they say and ask if you are understanding them right. "What do you think about that," and "Hum, interesting," will go a long way. These "Solution-Focused" questions are usually open ended and can help a kid process out their own solutions, rather than being told what to do. Often, young people don't want to be given the answers, because what do parents know anyway? Listening will always work on your relationship, even when they seem to prattle on and on, like a toddler, about stuff you can't even understand, but nodding and asking questions and making eye contact will show the respect they want and need from you and model good social behavior for them. It also might drive you to drink but gird your loins and hang on tight!

So yes, getting over can be growth-producing for the kid, and some things that go unknown are not going to hurt you as a parent and maybe gain points with a sibling. But when they do step over the line – and you as a parent need to decide and communicate where your bottom lines are – there needs to be the accountability. How do you feel about: Smoking, shoplifting, porn access, religious exploration, ear piercing, tattoos, punk rock, dating, sex, neon hair colors, midriff baring fashion, among other things? What are your values about these and what are your expectations of your kids. If you are wishy washy, your kids aren't going to know where the limits are, so they'll push the boundaries until you break.

I always find that car rides are good times to have formal talks about what I think is okay and what I think is not okay for them at their ever-changing ages. A family meeting around the table is also a good time to lay it all out there, and even take notes so everyone can agree to the decisions made. As kids get older, they want more say – even perceived say – in the rules that govern their

lives. This is not the time to clamp down on them –
they'll only push back. Give them a little more freedom
with a little more responsibility along the way so they
have time to practice with trial and error where it won't
ruin everything. It is basically saying, "If you show me
you can take out the trash every week and get your other
chores done without me telling you, then you are
showing me you are responsible enough to go to the
movies with your friends by yourself." Ask them to rise
to the challenge, and they will.

Empathy

Preteens have a better capacity for empathy than they did
as children. The idea of empathy still holds true; it is
important for them to be able to imagine how it feels to
be someone else. The kid who is always being teased, the
kid who is insecure, the kid who gets embarrassed in
front of the whole class, even the kid who seems to be on
top of the world. Having empathy for others will help
them stick to their values when crunch time comes.
Having the self-esteem to speak up for someone in the
face of peer pressure is hard for them. There is especially
a lot of talk around snitching or tattling at this age –
they're expecting one another to cover for them even
when they make bad choices. If a child sees that a
classmate stole from the museum store on while on a
field trip, they are given the silent or not so silent code
that they are to keep that quiet, making them part of the
crime. I heard about another situation where two students
exchanged drugs in front of a third party kid who wasn't

111

involved. That is, until they made that third party a witness, and possibly an accomplice, with real consequences. What can kids do?

Remember limit setting? Kids can do this too. "If you don't want me to snitch, then don't involve me in your bad decisions." They can give the clear message that while their misbehavior is their business, once they involve someone else without consent, that code of silence will not be honored. This information can empower a kid to not feel helpless and fall victim to being bullied or drawn into more misbehavior by friends or peers. This blends right into accountability, peers can hold one another to higher standards sometimes better than adults can. If your kid doesn't want to shower? Their friends will tell them to because no-one likes how they smell. It tends to take care of itself.

Accountability

As we discussed in the Childhood chapter, discipline needs to make sense. In other words, the punishment needs to fit the crime. If your kid stays out later than the agreed upon time: "you stayed out too late when you knew what time you were supposed to be home. Next weekend, you are staying in." When they didn't do their chores: "You didn't do the dishes when it was your turn, now you will do the dishes the next two nights." There is no need to yell, get all bent out of shape, or think of creative and unusual punishments for the kid. They make the connection that not following through with their responsibilities does not pay off. When you let them off the hook, they learn that your rules do not matter and well you can imagine how that goes. Staying on top of all of these things is exhausting, but in time, you come home and the dishwasher is running, the trash was taken out, and the dog got a walk. Today was one of those days for me, so I am confident that this style really works. If this does not work as well, sit down together and write out expectations, get their buy-in and have them help decide what the consequences should be if they fail to hold up their end in the household. Children are not just freeloaders in a home, they are a part of the home, and should be treated like their contributions are important. Feeling like they belong to their family and home will help them find that feeling as adults when they fly off on their own.

As kids get older, they also want more freedom, as I said, they've got to show you that they are ready for that freedom. But they are also exposed to more adult content online, through their friends, and basically everywhere they go advertising with scantily clad women are screaming "sex sells!" to us all constantly. Boys and girls are both pressured to be sexy, and sexual, and strut their stuff in the school halls. Teachers and parents are increasingly faced with how to address some of the acting out, but often end up either doing too little or way too much. Both are driven by misinformation and/or anxiety and are both ineffective in the long run. Girls and boys are asked and ask to "send nudes" over text (a felony, people! That's a Federal Law, by the way). As parents, we'd like to prevent our kids photos from ending up on the pedophile websites that exist, and teach kids that even if they are taking pictures of themselves, transmitting photos of underage kids without clothing for sexual purposes is illegal. I'm not talking about your toddler in the bath to grandma photos.

Kids also learn to use their physical power and sexuality for a purpose. Boys learn early on that they are physically stronger than girls and can overpower them, or even threaten to. Girls learn to use their "feminine wiles" to seduce and distract if there is a purpose. Genders do have different motivations for these behaviors; neither of which are socially acceptable. Both behaviors need to be called out similarly to how we addressed sexual play with children:

> Adult: Johnny, I saw you grab Suzie's bottom in the hall.
>
> Johnny: Nuh-uh, I didn't do that.
>
> Adult: Johnny, Suzie told me and I saw you with my own eyes. It made me feel uncomfortable and it made Suzie really angry. You will sit out of recess today as a result of your bad choice.

With a girl, the response isn't very different:

> Adult: Cara, you are standing too close to me, it is making me feel uncomfortable.
>
> Cara: Oh really, what do you mean (moving closer)?
>
> Adult: Step back, I just told you that it makes me uncomfortable and you moved closer. You need

to stop doing that, you will sit out of recess today as a result of your bad choice.

You name the behavior, how it makes you feel (or the person involved) and give the consequence right away. In other words, communication, empathy and accountability to address any early offenses that arise. I chose loss of recess as a consequence that makes sense because it keeps them from having physical contact with peers for a while, and in the line of sight of the adults. In the next chapter, I will talk about even more difficult scenarios that haunt all parents' worst nightmares, but that does not mean worse things cannot happen in the middle school years. I am just pacing us through this. Are you making connections yet? The point is to address these kinds of behaviors now in childhood before your kids grow up to be a creepy, grabby, narcissistic jerk who sees nothing wrong with being a creep? We know these things are going on based on the "Me Too" movement alone. It's clearly a problem.

Depending on where you live, what is illegal at what age may vary a bit. Generally, the following behaviors are considered against what is acceptable if not illegal:

> Voyeurism: peeping on others who are dressing, toileting

> Frotteurism: Rubbing or friction on another person for sexual purposes

> Indecent Exposure: Public nudity or showing another person sexual body parts

Sexual Harassment: Creating a hostile environment through innuendo, threats, bullying

Sexual Abuse: touching another person for sexual gratification without consent, either by a peer or adult

Rape: Non-consensual sexual intercourse, with or without use of force, violence

Encouragement

Just like young kids, older kids need to be (and want to be) acknowledged. We use similar language to let them know that they are seen, appreciated, and valued. Even if they are making mistakes left and right, moody and mean, are constantly needing to be grounded, it doesn't mean they are worthless. They are still doing something worthy of notice. Please notice, and not in a sarcastic, eye rolling, snickering way. "You have a way with fashion," could be said to a kid who is experimenting with their personal style. "I noticed that you fixed up the couch cushions, thanks." When they do something around the house without being asked. "I like spending time with you," even if you are on a trip to the drug store to get toilet paper. Also recall times when they did something right before but are resisting now, "I thought you enjoyed going to that class? You're always so happy when you get home and you learned so much."

You want to encourage anything that could lead to a new connection with them, a window into their thoughts and motivation. "You saw a funky skirt in a magazine? Can you show me so I know what to keep my eyes out for?" You might think that encouraging fashion or interests that you think are a bit wild and crazy will make your kid act out more... except it is just the opposite. When kids know that they are loved and valued even if they turn up with purple hair and combat boots one day, or tell you that they are gay, or that they might want to join the military instead of going to college, they are trusting you with their inner world. Nothing is set in stone so sit back and listen, ask questions, show love and let the future play out each day a little at a time.

Revenge

Revenge is one of the four STEP goals of misbehavior. It's an easy one to recognize because it makes us really mad and it also hurts. We say no to something, they turn around and say, "You're the worst mom ever," or something like that. Make no mistake, your kids know you well and will find the insult that stings the worst. Don't take the bait! You don't want to start insulting them back, "Why you little, ungrateful, brat!" and so on. You are smarter than they are. Say you spot that funky skirt while out picking up a gift at the mall, and it ends up being $450, retail. If that is in your budget and you're feeling generous, well that is your business. But most parents of middle school aged kids would practically faint at that price tag. They're liable to outgrow it before the year is over! So you try to break it to your child gently, "ouch, that's just not something I can afford, I'm sorry." Your child can agree that $450 is too much or say, "What? You said you'd get it! You never get me anything nice, I hate you!" And for the next hour they are sulking, rolling their eyes and sucking their teeth whenever you talk. You don't have to respond to them right away.

Let them experience the disappointment, it won't kill them. You can say, "I wish I could buy you that skirt, and I know you're mad, but I have to be responsible with my money." Just leave it at that. Behave as though it is all over. When your child comes to you later acting normal, go with it. If you child is still sulky, act as if everything is over. Don't let it get under your skin. You do not have to accept every argument you are invited to. Why would you argue with a child? You are in control of your emotions and behavior. Show them what that looks like.

Acting Helpless

The antidote to a kid pretending to be incapable or refusing to try is encouragement. But before you try that you might want to lose your mind at your kid. What do you mean you "can't? Do you want to fail the seventh grade?" Because god-forbid, what will you say to your friends if they do? Your child is looking for a reason to back out of a commitment, get you to do their work, your child may have been triggered and is in the "poor me" phase of their high risk cycle. This is an opportunity to sit down and wait. Yes, just wait. A simple, "let's talk about what's really going on?" let's them know you're onto this trick. Just be with them, they'll sigh heavily and maybe cry with a "you don't understand," and of course you don't – they have not told you anything. Some ways to manage feeling overwhelmed:

1. Break down the task into smaller steps or time periods
2. Point out what they have already accomplished
3. Help define what "finished" looks like
4. Notice how awesome the work they're already done is (even if it needs work)
5. Make sure they have the materials they need to do the task (paper, presentation board, markers)
6. Help create an environment where they can focus

Again, don't take the bait, don't join in the "poor me" talk. You'll know that this is the situation when you start feeling like nothing is going to get better, or that your child might just be incapable. That's when you need to take charge and turn it around. The expectation is still that they have to do the work, the chore or whatever it is that they are worried about doing. They want it to be perfect, and that's okay except, it may not be "perfect" according to an unreasonable standard. Help them figure out what finished will look like when it is truly finished. A third grade book report will no look like a bestselling novel, but if it meets the assignment's criteria and the child put good effort into it, that's great.

Violence

As your child gets bigger, you might realize that they have a physical advantage over you, over a sibling, friends, teachers. Sometimes adults get truly frightened by a large statured person, no matter what the age even if they turn out to be the gentlest, kindest person anyone could hope to meet. Add in a little racism, the large person has brown or black skin? Even the cops are "scared." I won't get side-tracked on this topic, but it holds a lot of truth. For the purpose of this book, we'll stick to parenting kids and preventing violence. How do we do it when violence is everywhere? Kids have gone from playing with toy soldiers, to GI Joe dolls, to playing video games where the more blood and guts the better. Western culture – mainly American culture – is gun focused as well. The proliferation of firearms doesn't help promote peace, I am sad to say. Often when I talk about preventing abuse while parenting, the assumption is that I am talking about preventing parents from abusing their children. Of course I want that, but what is different about this book, is that it is about preventing your child from becoming abusive.

What makes our jobs as parents extra hard, is finding a way to limit violent images, stories, experiences as well as keeping access to guns very limited. I get if you are a police officer, your child will see you with a gun, and is aware that there is a gun in the home. You are obligated to take all of the necessary precautions to keep the child from gaining access to the gun. Children are fascinated by guns, because of what they see in the media, so if they know where you store it, chances are they'll go looking for it. Be sure that it is locked up and the ammo, key or combination is kept in a separate location. Safety education is probably also a priority for you, and thank you for that. However, you could have a child with a serious mental illness who has paranoid delusions of killing – but if they have no access to a firearm or weapon, they aren't likely to do anything serious. They need mental health care, for sure!

If you have a child who is struggling with thoughts of violence, access to violent images is also going to need strict limits. Time and time again, I see kids in my office where parents are concerned about their behavior getting more violent, but all the child wants to do all day is play violent video games. I know it sounds simple: take away the games! But the push back from both parents and kids is intense. For kids, the pushback is obvious – they love the games, they'll be bored without them. They even get a "high" from the stimulation many games provide and giving up any kind of "drug" is going to take time. For parents – they don't want to do the work. The kid will get mad, nag for hours about the game, they'll have to find other things for the child to do with their time, so they give in.

Now let me be clear: violent video games do not cause violent behavior. To be honest, lashing out usually comes from fear, paranoia and feelings of worthlessness. If you have guns in the home – secure them well. Those feelings don't cause lasting harm to anyone on their own. Same for securing alcohol, drugs (do I even have to say this? Yes. Yes I do), and pornography. By "securing" I mean under lock and key, although preferable not in the home at all. When we prohibit things that are highly pleasurable and throw in a much bigger, stronger kid than when they were a toddler? Parents are afraid and the kids know it. It's so easy to take the road of least resistance. This is hard and this is only going to make more work for you, moms and dads. This is not a quick-fix-do-this-and-everything-will-be-great kind of book.

If your child has already done some high-risk things, you must find a therapist for them right away. Any sudden and dramatic change in your child's mood or behavior should alert you that something changed. You may be compelled to get them help through probation or the criminal justice system, but it would reflect better on you if you did it first. This is an age where sometimes kids are just in "the wrong crowd," and want to experiment, or they are struggling with mental health worries, and/or to be frank with you – you are not being the parent that they need. When you do not hold your child accountable, they learn that you don't care and they can do what they want. They don't think about the consequences, and they're subconsciously hoping that you might actually pay attention to them.

This is not to advocate for "helicopter parenting," letting them trip and fall is one thing, letting them go off a cliff is plain wrong. On the other hand, sending your child to a therapist to be fixed, or even sending them to a residential program without doing any work on yourself, is a set up. You are going to have to work on yourself. Since you are reading this book, I am hopeful that this is the start of something great for you.

Summary:

1. Middle Schoolers are full of hormones and angst. One minute they seem like children, and another minute they are demanding full independence from you.

2. Middle schoolers still want attention and acceptance from their parents; they are not ready to be pushed out of the nest.

3. Middle schoolers need to learn communication, empathy and accountability wherever possible.

Now You:

1. What are my values, and what values do I want to instill in my child/children as they grow up?
2. What are my child's/children's strengths?
3. What are areas of need for growth for my child/children?
4. Where do I as a parent need to let go, and where do I need to put in more time for my child/children?

"Never lend your car to anyone to whom you have given birth."

- Erma Bombeck

Chapter 6

The Teen Years

I cannot tell you how many times people told me, when my children were little, to brace myself for the teen years. I have two strong willed, good looking and bright daughters, and I was constantly getting the message that I could expect "trouble" when they become adolescents. Trouble from boys, attitude and acting out, sleepless nights and general bitchiness would define those years. Teens get a really bad rap for the minority of them that struggle and appear to be "bad." I'm living in a home that is rife with Estrogen – hopefully giving mine a boost – as well as big dreams.

I'm not gonna lie and tell you that it is a peaceful oasis from the debauchery from the real world, because well, that would be a lie. There is screaming, cursing, crying, falling on the floor in what I can only equate to a hangry toddler's tantrum, willful deceit, testing, moping, sibling rivalry, you name it, we got it. In the United States alone, there are on average 50 million high schoolers in the 21,500 high schools with an average of 526 students per school. You can't ignore them, or their problems. You may also want to know that on average, 85% of white students will graduate high school, while only 72% of Black and Hispanic students, and 78% of Asian/Pacific Islander students will graduate. We know that by now, graduating with a minimum of a high school diploma will help your teens live successfully. This is not the time to cut back on your involvement.

I happen to like teenagers, so you don't scare me! When I became a caseworker in my early twenties, I worked with a caseload of kids in foster care, some newborn, and some adolescents who were going to "age out" of the system. I think it helped that I was young, and had not yet forgotten what being young and unsure of everything felt like. I thought "the professionals" expected way too much from them – too much ability to make mature decisions, most often. As if I was supposed to tell them "don't do that, do this," and they were supposed to listen and everything would be okay after that. Of course I had a favorite, for so many reasons she was a lot of people's favorite.

When I met her, she was fifteen, and I was 23. She had been suspended for fighting and came to my office to meet me for the first time, and also talk about what happened in school. She was loud, quirky, stylish, and 100% Jamaica Queens. Mind you, this was not how she was described to me before I met her. I learned pretty fast that I tended to be more positive about my clients. By the time she left, she went from plotting her revenge to planning to stay away from the other girl and getting on with her life. And we clicked; she was like a lot of girls

I had known in high school. I'd meet her for lunch and talk, I'd slip her a little cash, walk around her neighborhood where we had more privacy. Once when she ran away, I took an agency car and drove around her neighborhood hoping to spot her, for several hours. By the time I moved on in my career, she had found her final home. I now know her through social media and she is also a woman in her 40s with a son, happily remarried, and also has her Master's in Social Work. If I had some kind of make-your-dreams-come-true fund to give away, she'd be on that list.

Another myth that gets attributed to teens is that they no longer want to spend time with their parents, or to be hugged, and seen with them in public. I know there are situations where parents go out of their way to embarrass their kids – like the dad who would take their daughter to the school bus in a different Halloween costume every day, or go to parties and dance like they dropped an ice cube down their pants. I often say that it is our job to embarrass our kids, but not to humiliate them. We do this by being silly, or sometimes just by being our doofy, IDGAF selves in public, simply because teens need to know that you can't be "cool" all the time. It's exhausting. I'll occasionally bust a move on line at the store and look up to a mortified face of my teenage daughter who was shaking her head, ever so slightly at me and mouthing, "please don't." Her little sister, will join me and we'll start singing to the overhead music, not even attracting any attention, but winning at the game of life. If this isn't your personality, there is no need to force yourself to be anything but yourself, as long as everything you do is honest.

Your teen still wants to be in a relationship with you. They do want affection and hugs, they just don't want it ambush-style while they are walking into their high school and all of their friends are waiting for them. Have a little respect, a little restraint, keep the smothering at a minimum and they'll respond in kind. The relationship, while being a lot less physical than when they were little, is very important. This is not the time to hand them a set of keys and some money and tell them you'll be in Bali for the next three years. Not that Bali is a bad idea... anyway I digress. Adolescence has some very specific developmental tasks that require a lot more complicated guidance than holding hands while they learn to walk.

Teens are going to be faced with a lot of pressures, questions, decisions, moral dilemmas. You don't have to have the answers, either. In fact, all you have to do is listen and ask questions. If you have ever coached a team, or supervised someone at work – it becomes a lot more like a professional relationship than parental. You are still the boss, but you are going to have to let go of some of that authority over time. Birds may know how to fly the minute they fall out of the nest, but humans need a little more practice.

You surely could not be so old that you don't remember what it's like to be a teen. You want to be free, but you want your parents to always take care of you. Your child believes deep down that they can't do anything because they aren't the ones with any money or any way to make money to take care of their needs. Many times, they are scared to ask for things they need because it always seems like they need something and parents go, "you need money again?" Remember all that? That hasn't changed since the dawn of time. You are also going to need to take one gigantic "Chill Pill" on a daily basis. I don't mean use drugs to deal with parenting a teenager or two, this ain't the '60's. This means, you need to calm down, listen more, react less, ask questions, then listen more without interrupting, second guessing, shutting down the conversation, issuing ultimatums. When your heart is walking around in a gangly, teenage, fast growing body, this is extra hard to do. They want to do the right thing, avoid disappointing you, then move away and leave you; but they'll be gone faster than you can roll your eyes if you can't hold your tongue long enough for them to speak a full sentence. This brings us back around to communication.

Communicating with Teens

You might not think, at first, that talking to a teenager is any different than talking to your child when they were small. Imagine, if you will, doing just that. How effective do you think your messaging will be if you are treating your teen the same way you treated them as a 6 year old? Kids grow up and parents must grow and mature right alongside them, because if you don't you're going to have to legally evict them from your basement when they are 40. Seem obvious enough but since this very scenario has happened in the world, um, let's get ahead of this one shall we?

Your teen's brain is much more mature at 13-18. By now you've been able to leave them to watch a movie while you go meet friends for dinner, or let them wander the shopping mall with a friend or sibling while you do errands. You may be hoping they make good choices, however, actively communicating your expectations for their good behavior in advance of a future outing is preferable. Your child will most likely bring up the topic, "Mom, can Josie and I walk around together without you at the mall this weekend?" What do you think, parents? Where is your mind going right now? Are you picturing them flirting with groups of boys walking around? Being lured into a van and whisked away? Eating too much junk food? There are a lot of choices to be made and you can negotiate many of them, as well as decide what you are not willing to negotiate. For example: "You two can walk around but you may not go to any of the separate buildings, and we meet back here at 3 o'clock."

Limits around their freedom not only help you manage your fears, but gives them boundaries in case a group of other kids does want to invite them someplace while you are busy. That way they can think, "that is beyond the limits," rather than wondering if you'd mind and going anyway. Of course if they were scared to say no, it never hurts to just blame the parents – they're gonna blame you for a lot worse anyway! "Sorry, my mom said I can't," is a quick and dirty escape from a potentially uncomfortable situation. They show that they can make good choices, little by little, and in turn, earn more opportunities to be out in the world. The clearer you are, the clearer they will be.

Offering a choice to a teen falls a bit more into the gray area than it would have when they were toddlers. They are busy people after all, teenagers. They've got homework, sports, dates, and often jobs to work around. So, if you want them to take out the trash in time for the garbage truck to pass by your place, you'll need to prepare: "Jack, the trash is getting full and the pick-up is tomorrow morning. Sometime before pick up would you please take the trash out?" Please and thank you. This shows that you respect their time and they don't have to jump up from whatever they were doing at that moment to do your bidding. They want to feel like they get to decide when they will do what you asked and usually, they want to think it is their idea.

Of course there will be times you can't give choices, like any other time in their life. If you dropped a glass and you need them to grab the broom for you before someone gets a shard in their foot, they had better to hop to it. You may have to be the bad guy, and a lot, and there will be days when they don't like you, appreciate what you are doing, and refuse to talk to you. They don't have to like you, and you will have to get over that if you are going to have a teenager. If you spend your time giving in to their demands because you want to be liked, you're in trouble.

What you can do instead is communicate your reasons, briefly, even if it is just to state firmly, "That is my final decision, this discussion is over." Get off the carousel of crazy already and stick to your resolve. If you feel you are doing what is right, even if "the other parents are allowing it," then own it. Their discomfort and feelings of self-pity are temporary and they will survive. Remember our "I" statement from Chapter 4? These still come in handy. In fact, they should by now have become a standard part of your vocabulary (if you happen to be reading this as your child grows into the stages, ha ha).

The format is I (emotion) when you (behavior) because (result or reason).

Let's say Annie keeps pestering her parents about saying no to the big party all the other kids are going to. Parent: "Annie, I feel irritated when you continue to ask me about that because I already gave you my final answer." Bye, girl, go sulk in your room. She may later discover that the police raided the party and several kids were charged with underage drinking. She may never thank her parents for keeping her home that night, but she might think it. It does not even matter.

Annie may later think it's cool to be passive aggressive about having been denied the party of the year, then what? She is in her cycle – the high risk cycle from

Chapter 4! She's being mean to her siblings, she's isolating in her room with the music turned up, she's refusing to speak to her parents directly, and on and on. This revenge seeking behavior is a great challenge for your parenting chops, right here. I personally love a good challenge, but not the kind you might be thinking of. When you have had enough of these shenanigans, you bust into her room... no, not that. When you have had enough, you go to her. She won't like you going into her room. But you go in, you turn off the music and you sit down on her bed, or chair if there is one.

> "Annie, in this family, we do not give each other the silent treatment because we are mad."

This is where you begin. You are reminding her that first and foremost, she is a member of the house and family and she knows better. Then you tug on her heartstrings a little by acknowledging her feelings, "Annie, I know you are angry that you didn't get to go. I know you are worried that your friends think you aren't cool. I have to make decisions that I think are right and will keep you safe." You can wait at this point, for her to say something, and engage in a reasonable discussion. No yelling, or going back into circles about *what ifs* and *you don't trust mes*. Go on with life as if everything is okay and continue parenting her. Tomorrow is a new day.

High Risk Behaviors

The last trigger warning – you must be expecting it by now. This is the reason why we get the warnings about adolescence, why people think it is going to be really hard. They are either projecting or expecting your teens to screw up. Maybe because those doomsday people had teenagers or were teenagers who made really bad choices back in their day. What I can tell you is that what you expect to happen, will generally happen. When you expect your pretty daughter to be "a heartbreaker" or even get pregnant while in high school; or your son to "be a manly man" they tend to live up to what they believe you mean. Your expectations are powerful, be mindful of what you say out loud.

What are some of the ways teens can be abusive? They are much more knowledgeable than children or middle schoolers, so frankly, things can get ugly. Recall that abuse can be harm to--

> Self: cutting, using drugs and/or alcohol, smoking
> Others: Emotional abuse, bullying, physical abuse, dating violence, harming animals, sexual abuse
> Property: Graffiti, theft/shoplifting, vandalism

We address high risk behaviors in the same format as in the past. You may find that when you call out the specific behaviors, you have to say some uncomfortable things.

"Shawn, I saw you trip Joey in the hall, and Joey is angry about it. That is abusive behavior, it must stop and there will be a consequence."

Dismissive response: *Oh those guys were just playing around.*

"Terri, you kicked the dog, I heard the dog yelp in pain. That is abusive behavior, it must stop and there will be a consequence."

Dismissive response: *She just got mad at the dog, no big deal.*

"Sam, Cheryl told me you kissed her lips in the hall after she told you to stop. That is abusive behavior, it must stop and there will be a consequence."

Dismissive response: *Sam was showing her he likes her.*

How often do we hear the dismissive response from adults? I can tell you that it is way too often, behaviors are then reinforced and do not stop. Having the language ready to address some of these examples that come up all the time can be a life saver. All too many adults, parents and non-parents believe that some form of mischief is a rite of passage. And you may recall that I suggested that some "getting over" on parents is a part of growing up. However, when the "mischief" involves abuse to another person, property or themselves, it must be addressed, and very specific to what the behavior is. I do want to again caution parents from using the word "appropriate," to describe misbehavior.

Using the above format to talk to your teen can prevent worse behaviors, which is my main point, overall. Sadly, teens do commit worse offenses such as grand larceny, selling drugs, sexual assault and rape. If your teen is being charged with a serious offense especially one that involves abuse, accountability from you, as well as the system is going to be a critical part of their recovery. There are a lot of debates currently about whether or not someone can be rehabilitated, especially when discussing sex crimes. Adults are generally considered dangerous by that point, because, as I said, by the time they are caught, they have quite a history of abusing others. Unlike other crimes, sexual crimes are highly physically reinforcing. That means, it feels good to them, for some pretty obvious reasons, which makes them want to repeat the behavior. If you can't imagine pairing sexual feelings with abusing another person, kudos! It is a terrible combination.

Back to teens – if your son or daughter is caught as a young person there is an extremely high likelihood that they will benefit from treatment! Why? Because they have young, immature brains and they will soak up the information and care and be more open to adapting. The more parents and other caregivers and informed supervisors can support the teens care, the better their chances.

Informed Supervision

The process of supervising a teen who has committed a sexual offense and is either adjudicated or on probation, is called informed supervision. That means the adult is informed of the teens offenses and risk factors. To be designated as an informed supervisor, you must believe that there is a reason for the services. Parents who deny the possibility of their children offending risk the chance of having their child placed outside of the home. You need to be all in on this one. Your child needs you more than ever; we must love our kids even when they do something terrible. This will also mean helping to create and implement safety plans for your teen. I am including an example of one, below.

This kind of plan can be useful in a number of situations so I would encourage you to use one if you're having some issues with your teen's behavior. Some teens will need to be monitored in all areas of their lives, public and private, some may only need supervision when around other teens, and some may be prohibited from being around younger children at all. Teens undergo an in-depth evaluation to determine what their risk factors are, and this may also involve a polygraph or "lie detector" test to assist an evaluator in discovering how deceptive the teen is being. The more honest a teen is, the better their chances in treatment. I am not going to go terribly deep into this process, because I am hoping that with this book you will be able to manage any high-risk behaviors well before anything this serious has to happen. Also, services will depend on where you are in the world; as we know, not all States or Countries have the same processes.

Safety Plan examples:

Behavior: Kenny becomes angry and throws household items at his siblings

Goal: Kenny will use alternative ways to express his anger that are healthy and safe.

> Tasks: Kenny will identify when he starts to become angry (red, hot face, stomach drop sensation, voice raised)
>
> Kenny will communicate his feelings to a safe adult (Mom, dad, grandfather) and ask for help
>
> Kenny will develop coping skills for anger such as deep breathing, taking a walk, writing in a journal, exercise, putting on calming music, playing with putty.

Goal will be met when: Kenny does not have an explosive outburst for 3 continuous months.

Consequence for subsequent episodes: Kenny will lose one week of video games.

Reward for one week of no outbursts: Kenny will go to a movie with a friend.

Behavior: Kenny (yes let's keep picking on Kenny) has been smoking, using a vape and was caught drinking beer.

Goal: Kenny will not use or abuse substances while he is underage.

> Tasks: Kenny will become educated on the laws around buying and using tobacco products and alcohol.
>
> Kenny will turn over any and all smoking products and paraphernalia to parents.
>
> Kenny identify triggers to wanting to use smoking and drinking products.
>
> Kenny will learn alternative ways to cope with triggers and urge to use (similar to above).
>
> Kenny will no longer spend time with peers who smoke and drink, and find peers who do not.

Goal will be met when: Kenny no longer wants or uses tobacco or alcohol products for 3 months.

Consequence for subsequent use: Kenny will lose allowance for a week.

Reward for one week of no use: Kenny will earn a Starbucks gift card of $5.

Parents can engage their teens in helping to be a part of the solution, getting their buy-in. Teens want help; they realize that their behavior is problematic and is interfering in their relationships, they don't like feeling out of control and getting in trouble. When a teen is able to make their own safety plans – which could be a simple mental note like: *That kid always triggers my anger, so I am going to walk down another hallway to get to class so I don't pass him*, then you know they have "graduated."

Again, the steps are the same as for younger children, you are only relating now to someone more mature.

1. Name the behavior specifically and how you know it is happening (you see it with your eyes, hear it with your ears).
2. Tell the child how it makes you (or the other person) feel.
3. Prohibit the behavior and add a consequence if needed.
4. Monitor for more behaviors.

Mental Health

Just as a teen can offend against someone, a teen can be the victim of an offender. We tell our kids to tell us, all the time, if there is anything going on, and we pray like sinners in church that they have nothing to disclose. If you have been a calm, attentive parent and your child's expectation is that you do not "freak out," when they tell you something they think might upset you, chances are your teen is being honest. But as I said earlier, people who hurt kids, especially the adult ones, are very good at "grooming" others and flat out terrifying the young people they wish to victimize. Even as adults they find it difficult to finally explain to their parents what really happened to them.

I am always shocked when I hear that parents did not know – because so often the child or teen's change in behavior was sudden, drastic and unusual. Perhaps because I am from an earlier generation, that young women and men were labeled as borderline and troubled when in fact they were abused and traumatized. I am grateful of how much more we know as a society, but it isn't enough to respond differently when we can prevent it from happening in the first place. We have the know-how! If your child won't talk to you – ask them who they would prefer to talk to, and go to that person, as soon as possible. Offer to find them a therapist and respect that relationship (i.e. don't pry into their discussions).

The suicide rate among young people is higher than ever, so anytime a child or teen says "I'm going to kill myself," it has to be taken seriously. The most recent statistic is that the suicide rate is as high as 14% among teens and young adults which is after a steady climb since the 1990's. It is not a good topic to make jokes about, it is not something to say lightly. I used to have a friend who said it all the time and I finally told her that I was starting to worry that she was serious. She said she was kidding and decided to try to find some other way to express herself when she was feeling frustrated. There are certainly times when teens say it to "get attention." Um... it concerns me that they had to go to this extreme, even so far as making an attempt through self-harm

Warning Signs:
Threats to commit suicide
Depression
Anger/Irritability
Loss or Lack of Interest
Changes in Appearance
Schoolwork worsens
Preoccupied with Death and Suicide
Previous Attempts
Making arrangements for belongings, plans

simply to get a parent to notice them, to notice that they are unhappy.

The good news is: It can be prevented! Kids respond to getting help and support. Lately, it has been more normalized and even glamorized in television shows as though it were a viable solution to problems. It is never a solution. Reducing access to firearms, keeping drugs and medications out of reach of all children, including teens, asking kids about suicidal feelings and talking directly about it also makes an impact. Adults need to work on those skills as well because it's scary and uncomfortable. Kids who are suicidal want to talk about it and it does not make it more likely that they will try to hurt themselves.

We have so much work to do, if teens are feeling like they are not getting the attention they need from the adults in their lives. If you see that your teen is wearing long pants and long sleeves all summer when it is 90 degrees out, pay attention. Many times they really just want to have time with you, moms and dads, where you are noticing how they are growing up, you are asking what they like, you are listening to them talk, you are telling them funny stories of when you were young and made foolish decisions so they can get to know you, too. This relationship can be incredibly preventative for future problems. They respect you when you hold boundaries and let them know when they have crossed the line. However, if your child is expressing suicidal feelings and/or cutting, making attempts, this has to be addressed by professionals. Most moms and dads are not equipped to manage this on their own, and it's okay to ask for help for you, too.

One of the standard responses after a hospitalization or a trip to the emergency room, is to put a teen on some medication. There is a short list of anti-depressant medications that are approved for this age group. It is not, however, the end of your worries. As a therapist, I have seen teens have wonderful responses to an anti-depressant. They are less anxious, they smile more, they are taking better care of themselves. But the chief complaint is that they feel "numb" after a while. Similarly, with children who have strong behavioral outbursts, the solution is to give them a dose of a heavy sedative so they can calm down. The problem with this is that they never learn to tolerate and manage intense emotions.

Children and teens feel out of control when they are angry, anxious, excited and afraid. Some can have reactions that don't make sense to the adults around them and they get labeled in school or at home as troublemakers or just "bad kids" or get a formal diagnosis of Oppositional Defiant Disorder. When we take the time to help them identify and name the feeling, why they are having the feeling, what they can do instead of throwing, breaking, screaming, hitting, insulting and go through it with them.

I like the concept of "time in" versus the "time out" approach with misbehavior. While it would appear that we are reinforcing "bad" behavior by giving it our attention, the relationship we build with our kids this way is priceless. When a child does have trauma, known or unknown, we give them the space to feel the feelings, learn to regulate their bodies again, talk about what they are feeling, and help them get through it. This is absolutely more work than sedating a child that we just don't want to deal with at the time. If you have to sit on the floor of the grocery store and do this, it's nobody's business but your own and this does not mean you are condoning their negative behaviors. Your child is worth every second.

Often adults struggle to understand why a teen would feel so depressed or anxious to the point where they might self-harm. We see them as being in the best years of their lives – they have no real responsibilities, no bills to pay, friends, school is easy. However, it is becoming more and more apparent that teens are just as stressed out by the "rat race" as adults! Forty five percent of teens surveyed by New York University, report feeling overwhelmed with responsibility. School, work, jobs, pressure to get into college and grades, leaves them feeling like they have little purpose to their day to day lives. Sadly many also reported maladaptive coping skills such as using alcohol and marijuana to relax. As parents, we need to demonstrate at home how to manage stress better. We are told in our jobs that the "work life balance" is important to avoid burnout, it is the same for kids! They need downtime, to listen to music, play (yes, they still want to play), exercise and do sports, to learn good organizational and time management skills. Schools also need to play a part – has your teen ever come home to say that all of their teachers scheduled a report due on the same day? They are given the response that it's how life goes in the real world. It does not have to be this way. Perhaps you and a few other parents can make a difference by speaking to school administrators about helping to reduce stress.

Sexuality

Now where were we? Oh yes, get comfortable, regulate yourself, clear your mind, once again. You may have gotten the impression from me that all sexual contact between teens is abusive. That's a no, from me. Your teen, just like when they were younger, has a sexuality, either emerging or decided. They are considering their options, like, all the time, because their hormones are taking over. Have you given some good thought to the earlier questions about your values? If not, please do that. What we want, for them, and for humanity, is to be healthy, to be loveable, to be able to love, to respect others, to have empathy and be able to read social cues accurately around sexuality. And to be safe – safe from others, safe from making poor choices.

Imagine how much healthier a society we could be living in, if all of us grew up safe, respected, not seeking constant validation from others because we don't know ourselves? Or because we have been harmed at some point while growing up? I have stated this, way back at the beginning, that adults who do harm to others, more often than not, started abusing others as children or as teens. Imagine if those adults, had nurturing parenting, communication, empathy and accountability as children. If your child has hurt others, or has been hurt already, there is help. And best of all, there is prevention.

There is prevention from abuse, prevention from sexually transmitted infections, prevention from unplanned pregnancies. Parents and professionals need to be able to have open, honest, and accurate dialogue with teens about sexuality. Ideally, our kids will wait until they are a little older – in the early adult phase of life. The decision to engage in sexual behavior is much more of an adult decision than a kid decision. I try to tell my children and my clients that they have so much time, there is no hurry, to just make friends and focus on relationship skills without the physical part just yet. They all talk about how much pressure there is, how easily girls can get a reputation for being promiscuous or a prude. Still, after all these years. That boys are still driven by their desire and are trying to have as much sex as they can while they can as if the world were ending.

What matters is how clear they are on what their parents think about sex in the teen years. I have heard some parents say, "I don't want you to have sex, but if you do use a condom." Okay that's great that you want them to be safe, but it's a pretty confusing message, even if it is completely true! Do you not want them to have sex, ever? You don't have control over when they do it, but you can let them know your expectations and give them things to think about.

> Are you ready or are you being pressured to be ready?
>
> Are you in a trusting, mutually caring relationship?
>
> Have you thought about what kind of birth control you are going to use? Do you need help getting it? Do you need more information?
>
> Are you aware of all of the consequence like infections and pregnancy and how to prevent them?
>
> Do you think you are in a good place in life to be in this level of a relationship?

Also, where are they planning to "do it?" How do you feel about them having sex in your house? In their beds? Would that be preferable over the backseat of someone's car or late at night in the local baseball dugout? I can't answer for you. You aren't obligated to make this easy for them, either. Taking them to the doctor as a teen is a little different than when they were kids because you will be sent out of the room. This seems to start around age 13. I was initially surprised by being told I had to leave the first time, and I was also cut off from seeing my child's record. I knew that there was nothing at that time that I should not see, but I also know that there are a lot of teens out there who don't have a parent who is nurturing and flexible. Obviously, doctors have the most information about birth control and infections, and teens feel comfortable discussing these things most when their parents aren't listening. They don't want to disappoint you, embarrass you or feel embarrassed, so I get it. This policy was not in place when I was a teen and I remember wanting to be able to speak for myself.

Of course there is always a chance that despite your efforts and good intentions, your child becomes pregnant or impregnates a girl much earlier than anyone wanted. While parenting is lovely, it really does take a mature adult who is ready to be a parent to do it well. If you don't want your child to find themselves in this situation, please re-read the above, like 100 more times. The conversation is uncomfortable but the more you do it, the easier it gets. You also will need to take your child to the doctor where you will be kicked out and the young woman and hopefully her partner, will get the "talk" on what they did and what they want to do about it. Can they see themselves as parents now?

At the time I write this, access to abortion services is being curtailed in many of the Southern States such as Georgia and Alabama. This means, your children may not get services there, or even birth control services, limiting your ability to make good choices for your family. In the end, it is up to the person who will grow, birth and feed the baby from her body, to decide what happens to her body. You may not think it's right, but again, there is so much we cannot control.

When I mentioned *emerging sexuality*, I meant that your teen has sexual feelings but also that there is a chance your child is gay. I know it might seem like "all of a sudden" there are all these gay folks living out and proud. What you might not realize is that there have *always been* gay people, who knew it when they were quite young, but did not live in a world where they would be accepted and loved if they showed it openly – or it was flat-out illegal. So they hid their true selves and were often pretty miserable.

Acceptance from parents is doubly important for these kids, we know that gay/lesbian/trans/questioning teens are three times more likely to attempt suicide than heterosexual teens because of the difficulty factor, and they only make up about 5% of the population in the United States. If your child is gay, he or she didn't "become" gay from anything you did. Similarly, there isn't anything you can do to change them or "cure" them. It is not a disease that requires a cure, and sadly there

149

have been "treatment centers" operating that have literally tortured too many teens while promising to cure them of their "unnatural" desires. What they need is your love and support, the same as every other day of their lives. It does not change what we should want for our kids – healthy relationships, solid values, education, a kind disposition and personality. If they have those things you've done an amazing job!

This generation of teens has another thing that I did not have, nor basically anyone earlier than me: technology. By now, most of us have a smart phone that connects to the internet, has more sophisticated graphics than NASA, helps us make friends all over the planet, and sadly has proliferated child pornography and human trafficking, making kids more vulnerable than ever. In the old days, of when I was a teen, we were strongly warned against "dirty old men" asking us to pose nude, as well as the warning that nude photos could turn up any time and "ruin" our lives. Now I think the human body is a beautiful thing, and being exposed with a photo of yourself from when you were young, and probably more beautiful than you ever appreciated at the time, shouldn't necessarily ruin your career or chances to advance. For teens, taking and sending nude selfies or photos of friends changing clothes can result in serious charges.

Parents need to have this conversation, and often, about the seriousness of it. Even engaging in "innocent" and consensual "sexting" is a concern because it could progress to sending images. Kids get caught everyday feeling pressured, conned, extorted when they refuse to do what is asked. On the other hand, being on the receiving end of unrequested and unwanted images is upsetting as well. As the parent of a teenage girl, I know that teen boys are still asking, even when they are told no, they still ask. I can't help to be angry when I hear this because it seems so simple to just go "oh well I tried," and let it go. We can't leave it all to talking to our daughters to not "let" anyone take advantage of them. Girls need to be okay with being assertive, even being called "a bitch" when they set boundaries.

Boys absolutely need to be told and held accountable that even asking is rude, and when someone says no, accept that no as final. One day, perhaps when they are older, someone who loves them will surprise them with special pictures, but they are a gift, not an expectation.

Body Image

As I said, the human body is beautiful, and nothing is more beautiful to a parent's eye is their own perfect child. It can be painful to hear a child talk about their appearance in any way other than complete awe. We try our best to give them good food, exercise, positive reinforcement that they are beautiful. We must watch our mouths when we talk about our own bodies. When we were young, we were also beautiful, and we still are, we just get older, put on a little weight, get varicose veins and wrinkles. We cannot predict or control when this happens, try as we might. We have to learn to say nice things about ourselves. This isn't just when the kids can hear you – your ability to love yourself and demonstrate

151

that you love yourself will help your children love themselves as well. Growing up in a home where someone comments on your food, "If you eat that you'll get fat," or your body, "well I see you've been enjoying dessert," is devastating to the self-esteem of a young mind who already feels incredibly insecure.

Boys and girls receive images every day of perfection. It used to be in advertisements and magazine layouts. Now it is on Instagram and Snapchat, and everyone is filtered to look unearthly, smooth and perfectly made up; and the trends will come and go in terms of what body is preferred in media. The influence of these images is powerful and there is almost no 100% fool proof way to protect our kids from them. We can delay it, but not stop it. On this earth, there are no two bodies that are the same (not counting identical siblings). How can anyone say that one is more ideal than another? Those are the questions we need to ask our teens, when they make a disparaging remark about their looks or their body. If there is something they want to do – like lose a few pounds or bulk up with muscles, there are healthy ways to do it and those should always be encouraged. Good nutrition, an active lifestyle, safe workouts once they are old enough – usually 14 or 15 to safely use gym equipment – can help them achieve their goals. Setting goals for anything is a useful way to reach important milestones in life. Speaking of goals, we are gonna look at how to help your teens figure out what they want to do "when they grow up…"

Goals

One of the most common sources for anxiety in people who want to achieve anything is how to set a goal. We tend to see the final result in our mind – usually of ourselves rolling around in a pile of cash and we have no idea how to get there. To get to the magic coast, we have to hike through the desert, climb the mountain, battle the troll under the bridge, avoid the enchanted forest... these are the steps involved. There are always more than we realize.

Teens usually want to move out into their own place and be independent, and are overwhelmed by the task. They want to go to college, they want to get a job, or save for a car. These are really big for someone to achieve without a plan. So how does a goal oriented person begin? There are several options:

The accepted way to write a goal is the SMART format. And yes, if I am your therapist, I will have you write it down someplace. I also encourage parents to help their teens to do the same. They can write in a journal, a white board, the bathroom mirror - if that is where they will see it.

S: Specific. What are you trying to achieve? The result of your efforts.

M: Measurable. How are you going to quantify your success and progress? In terms of money? Lowering or increasing scores on a test?

A: Achievable. If your goal is to grow wings and fly away then you're just setting yourself up.

R: Realistic. You aren't going to play professional basketball if you are only 5' tall. But you may have other options for your talents.

T: Time limited. What time frame are we looking at? What date are you aiming for?

You might notice that the safety plan earlier in this section is in this format. It can be used for almost any topic. So here is an example based on the above breakdown:

GOAL: Get accepted to college
Tasks/action steps
- Complete all school assignments in class and at home.
- Maintain a B or better grade point average.
- Attend school daily.

- Take the SAT or ACT when the test is offered – Junior year. Join a study group.
- Research which schools would be a good fit for my interests. DUE DATE:
- Apply to 1 reach school, 1 safety school, and 3 schools that I could reasonably get into. DUE DATE:
- Research scholarships and grants, discuss with school guidance office. DUE DATE:

Another way to set goals is to break them down into time frames. Listing those in a grid format can also help break them down and prioritize. What do you want to or have to get done in the next 30 days? 6 months? 1 year and 3 years? You're making 4 boxes and sometimes the tasks and goals will be moved up or moved farther out depending on what is going on in your life.

The next 30 days Save an extra $20/week Research cars I can afford	The next year Maintain car/find good shop Consider new job or promotion with pay increase
The next 6 months Shop used cars with dad Get license and insurance information Buy car	The next three years Upgrade car Sell first car

Another creative option is the vision board. There are many tutorials online about these. If you are unclear of what direction you want to go it, doing one of these may assist you in determining a course of action. These are usually done with images that represent what you would like to see happen in your life. It's also a wonderful way to procrastinate! There are kids who seem to know exactly what they want to do in life – early deciders. Then there are other kids who don't seem to ever know or can't make a decision. Those are the kids we need to spend time with, helping them identify their interests and what a career in those interests might look like.

I mean, we might all like to video ourselves playing video games on YouTube for money... but that is also an actual job, like it or not. It takes energy, interest, investment in good quality equipment, and personality. There aren't a lot of careers out there that require zero initial work. Help your teen be realistic without totally shutting down any conversation about something you think might be ridiculous. If you are horrified, just hold your face still and say, "that sounds interesting, I'd like to know what you are going to do to make that happen." And see what happens. They might make something magical happen and you can brag about it for the rest of your days.

Many of the topics in the teen section can apply to the middle school section and vice versa. I said it in the beginning, and I'll say it again, often our biggest challenge in parenting is finding the right response to the right behavior at the right time. There is a lot to know and be able to spot when you are living in the moment and feeling all the feelings that come up when your child is doing all the amazing things they do. Obviously, there is no way to write a book that covers everything a child can do and be, but this can be a good start.

Summary:

1. Teens are not inherently bad, troublesome, or promiscuous.
2. Teens still want and need their parent's approval and attention.
3. Through relationship, teens can be influenced to succeed in school, set goals and achieve their dreams.

Now You:

1. What are your expectations around chores, friends, schoolwork, now that your child is older?
2. What do you remember about being a teenager and what would you like to see that is different for your child? What would you like to see that is the same?
3. Create a safety plan for a concerning behavior you have about your teen.
4. What boundaries are non-negotiable in your parenting? What are you willing to be flexible about?

When you become a teenager, you step onto a bridge. You may already be on it. The opposite shore is adulthood. Childhood lies behind. The bridge is made of wood. As you cross, it burns behind you"

-*Gail Carson Levine*

Chapter 7

Young Adults

You can only be a child once, and it only lasts for a short time, comparative to the rest of your life, if you survive to the average life span. And as the quote above suggests, there is no way to go back once you have crossed that bridge. The milestone from childhood to adulthood is critical, but it looks different for everyone. I don't know if everyone experiences the transition in the same way – that feeling one may get when they know they are a "Grown Up," through a job, a conversation, or a relationship. Being an adult is getting bad rap, if one looks at social media, for example. "Adulting" can be seen as triumphant – "I did my laundry and swept the floors today!" Or a great big pain that should be avoided at all costs – "I don't want to adult today, I am staying in bed."

I met another mom recently for after work drinks and we agreed that it was good to get out of the house, talk to another grown up. However when we said the word, "adulting," it did not seem to fit. I still haven't been able to come up with a term that is more fitting to our situation. We know how to be adults, but when you become parents, it's all you seem to do anymore. You have to be responsible, easily roused at 2AM when your ninja child is standing over you breathing loudly, get the bills paid, the house maintained and food put out on the table. We needed to meet up and not have to take care of anyone for a couple of hours.

If all goes well, you will put your child on to a train, bus, airplane, or into a car and with a good shove, okay I mean a gentle nudge, they will cross the threshold of their own life, no longer a child, and perhaps not quite an adult, but a person on their own. Don't deny that you fantasize about this day, but that you also find your eyes welling up with tears while trying not to start having hitching breaths controlling it. Your kids will also have some conflicting feelings – they want to be on their own just as badly. But if you live in New York, and they start school, a job, boot camp, in California, you will all feel the distance before you can stop hugging.

Maturing involves an inner journey that our kids go on, and if we are lucky, we get to see some of that happening. Just like you, when you found yourself evolving from a child into an adult, your child will also evolve. It can also mean that they realize that some parts of growing up appeared nicer than they were. That adults were not always honest, that the adults made mistakes, that they had less or more of what they were told they had. They are analyzing the adults around them – bosses, friends, the friends' parents as well. What does an adult look like? How do they behave? Even well into adulthood I would see a professional woman at work and think, "Wow that is how I want to sound when I speak in meetings." Encourage your young adults to be around people whom they admire and are like-minded. Again, listen to them, and ask questions such as, "What is it about that woman at work that makes her impressive to you?" and so on.

A relationship with your adult child is moving less and less toward "parenting" them, as it was in the teen years, and more and more toward friendship. The more you treat them with the respect and comradery that you give your best friends, the more they will want to call and visit. You are going to need their help as you progress into late adulthood – and grown up kids are good for rides to appointments and changing lightbulbs in the ceiling. Appreciate what you have got.

Independence also tends to involve the economy. When I graduated college in 1992, we were told not to expect to be able to live on our own right away – that jobs would be difficult to get and apartments would be expensive. That didn't turn out to be true in my case – I did get a job and I did find an apartment;

I simply did not want to live with my mom anymore so I made it happen. The same seems to be true now – only things have changed in the last 25 years: the incomes have not grown to match the expenses.

Kids are living at home, not because they don't want to leave, but because they can't afford to. I could go on a long tangent about how minimum wage is the same now as it was when I was a young adult, which is freaking outrageous, but let's assume right now that these things are not problems – that it is about your child's ability to budget, stay organized, and be emotionally mature, that will lead them to move out. I also realize that if your young adults are happy, contributing, and everyone gets along, staying home longer is a viable option. With good boundaries, it can be done. But generally speaking, we are raised to believe in Western cultures that our own homes are the goal. I am also writing from an assumption that your child first goes to college.

I am of the school of thought that college is a good transition from home dependence to independence. You are away from your parents, have to make choices for yourself, be responsible and have the pressure to support yourself 100% taken away. The experience of wanting freedom – that if your parents are paying for school you have to keep grades up, for example – can drive a young person to finish and move on. College is a choice, it is also reasonable to go to a trade school, the military, or straight to a job full time after high school. There are certainly a lot of people out there who have been successful without college.

As a parent, you may not like the path your child is on after school ends. You may expect college, and your child is hell bent on being a Marine, or the other way around. Pushing them to do something they cannot see themselves doing is a really great way to stress your relationship with them. If that is what you want, then by all means go ahead, but holidays might be lonely. They might have a job that you think isn't enough for their skills and talents. You may be right, but your child may be happy for the time being and you can have faith that your child will reach the point where they are ready to take a risk and move on. It is their life, it is no longer yours to dictate, only influence where you can. That's a tough place to be if you held strong desires for your child or children's future. Arguing with them about it is just chasing your tail.

 If you still don't understand why I am telling you this then I have failed. You can have a relationship with your child that is respectful, shows good communication, empathy and accountability. If you have done these things, your child will be okay. They may actually be happy, successful, interesting people.

Planning

I mentioned a few things we all need to do fairly well to be on our own, such as budgeting. It is a good idea to talk with your kids, starting much younger than now, about money. What does your child think about money? Is it scarce or do they think there is always plenty? What do you want them to think about money? If your kids are still young, what do you need to change about your money messaging so your kids believe they can have everything they want from life? If you child says, "I'm going to be lawyer because someday I want to be The President." What would you say? "Good luck with that," or "If you really want that, you can do that."

Your support and your language is everything. In order to be independent they should understand how much money they have day to day and how much things are going to cost. They need to know that the important things, like housing, food, transportation to work, are priorities, whereas going out for drinks and fancy sneakers are luxuries that they can have – after the bills are paid. How do we get them to understand this so they aren't showing up on your doorstep with their belongings and no place to go six months after leaving?

1. Open a bank account, if needed.
2. Have them list their income after taxes (learn to read a paystub).
3. Have them list their necessary expenses and deduct from their income.

4. Have them list their discretionary expenses and deduct from the remaining income.
5. Have them record every cent they spend – this can be done on a paper log, or an app for their phone. Knowing what they spend on bills and coffees helps them to budget and predict expenses better.

Will they have enough? Do they have a "cushion" fund saved for emergencies (easier to do before they have moved)? Are you, the parent, willing and able to subsidize them until they are "on their feet?" These are questions that you and your child will need to consider. I am neither pro nor con giving your young adult money, it just depends on your values and ability. It's your child's ability to use the money wisely that will matter the most. Being able to do this also encourages maturity and organization over time.

Skills

Other things we all need to know when we are first starting out: basic cooking, home maintenance like cleaning properly and taking care of issues promptly instead of letting them get worse until a crisis hits (like not reporting a leak to the landlord), making their own doctor and dentist appointments – and showing up to appointments on time. How to sew a button back on a shirt, do laundry, car maintenance basics, if they have a car. For many kids, these things happen over time since it's a lot better than a crash course as an adult. Schools used to send the boys to shop where they learned basic carpentry among other very useful skills, and girls to home economics to learn to be good little housewives. I would love to see these classes come back and offered to all high schoolers. If they do not yet possess these skills and you haven't been vigilant about teaching them, do their future roommates and partners a favor and get going on that one. No-one likes a slob or someone helpless sharing their space and needing to be re-parented. Balancing being a parent, a mentor, friend, will be a difficult transition for you. You can't control their lives, although you can still influence them and remind them of the values you tried to instill as they were growing up. They may not seem to listen, but they will remember. Always tell them that you believe in their abilities and trust their good judgement. They are now grown and don't need you to wipe their… faces, anymore.

Summary

1. Young adults will usually find a way to GTFO of your house.
2. Young adults will need to have developed some skills of independent living by the time they leave home.
3. Parents will need to balance support with the need to control their young adults.

Now You:

1. What do you remember about moving out of your family home as a young person? Did you make an escape? Or was it planned? What do you hope for your child?
2. List 3-5 things your young adult needs to improve before they would be ready to be independent.
3. How would you like to see your relationship grow when you are both older? What has been your relationship with your parent in adulthood?

Love is the most important healing power there is.

-Louise Hay

Chapter 8

Debriefing

When we reach the end of any book, there is a sense of accomplishment and sometimes, sadness, especially when a book has really touched our hearts or given us some inspiration to go out into the world and make good changes. Obviously, there are parenting concepts that are not in this book, just as there are topics in this book that aren't in any other book. I hope this book has given you some purpose and ideas for how you would like to see yourself as a parent in the coming years. I am aware that some of the topics in this book can be hard to get through – just as in some of the trainings I have done, parents have struggled to change their gut reactions during practice exercises and adopt new ways to handle tough situations. Some parents have become upset during trainings because of the feelings it brings up. I encourage you to go back often to the sections of the book that apply to your parenting dilemmas, until you find that it is a part of your daily language.

My dream, that I may or may not be around to see fulfilled, is to dramatically reduce, if not eliminate, the instances of child sexual abuse in the world. To do this effectively, is not to throw all the pedophiles in jail and throw away the key until the end of time. That is a reaction, not a response. What will change the world is to *prevent* anyone from becoming abusive, starting in childhood. That is something worth fighting for.

To recap here:

5. Name the behavior specifically and how you know it is happening (you see it with your eyes, hear it with your ears).
6. Tell the child how it makes you (or the other person) feel.
7. Prohibit the behavior and add a consequence if needed.
8. Monitor for more behaviors.

You may have found that you have been on a healing journey since becoming a parent, as many of us have. Being a parent does not mean repeating old patterns until the end of time. It can be a powerful means to change the world, in fact. Or, just change ourselves. We can only change ourselves, truth be told, and not others. We change how we respond to others instead, that changes others' behaviors. Knowing we are raising our kids differently, and often better, than we were raised helps us see the potential we might have had long ago, and watch it flourish through our children.

What in particular has stirred up your inner turmoil? For many it will be the issues around sexual abuse, having been victimized, wanting to be protective without locking up your child in a tower, or feeling as though you did not do enough to keep your child's behavior from escalating. You now have some skills to pass on, perhaps to a friend who is having similar issues, if not to your own repertoire of parenting skills.

I recently watched a documentary about children with mental illnesses called "Dangerous Sons," although it was about boys in particular. The one thing I found that was similar was the auto-responses of the parents. Some of the parents were trying to stay calm and factual with their sons, some simply became angry the minute their child became angry, and I don't want to single anyone out. Most of the boys in this show have developmental disorders as well as behavioral, which is doubly hard for anyone to manage.

I was more unimpressed with the professionals. The child would have an emotional response and the parents and therapists would completely ignore it. A child became frightened and no-one paid any attention to it. A child was angry and it was met with more anger. These are missed opportunities to stop and say, "You seem to be having a really strong feeling to this news, tell me about that," instead the children continued to feel invalidated and eventually escalated. The therapists, if present, would say nothing, or a child would get treatment but the parents did not. We need to do better, the mental health system is only a small part of helping kids do better. Parents are with their kids more than any other adult, and they need *all* the skills. For these kids with more difficult and severe behaviors, I strongly recommend the Beyond Consequences model, listed in the resource section.

The stakes have never been higher, and many of you are already aware of that. We need to be involved parents, no matter how exhausted or frankly disinterested we are in what they are doing. Even if you think you have nothing to offer your child, your time is everything to them. You can offer yourself and what you have learned, you don't need to lecture them like a teacher, or order them around like a Drill Sargent. They just want to be around you. Go to all the games they are in, be in the audience of all the school plays, attend every parent-teacher meeting you can, help with homework, stay up to date on the latest trends for their age groups. For this short period of time out of your entire life, you can do this.

Some of my feedback while writing was to add more stories. Honestly, I want to light a fire under parents' butts but I don't want to terrify you. I have stories that could give you nightmares for the rest of your life! I don't think that would drive home the lesson, or better illustrate the need for change. I know there are places in the world, some not too far away from me, that deny that these are problems, either because the experience is limited (thankfully) or that it is meant to be kept silent as a part of a more closed culture. Schools are discussing curriculums to help kids trust their feelings, know that predators will try to befriend them and how, when to talk to a trusted adult about concerns. Again, these solutions leave a lot to the children to do for self-protection. And we know that too many "trusted adults" are historically perpetrators of incredible abuses against children as well as adults. What would more stories really do to help you? All you need to do is believe that there is a problem, and that there are solutions.

What do you need to do now, to take care of yourself? If this book has made you realize that you need to do some work on yourself, then do it! What have you got to lose? Only everything – your relationships, your patience, your soft, tender heart, among a few things. Go out and get you some Brené Brown books, find a therapist, or join a parenting support group. The very act of engaging in some kind of self-awareness or improvement will have a lasting impact. The first step is the hardest and can be the most powerful. Reading a self-help book got me to sit down and write this book, so I know books can change lives.

Words for Feelings

Affectionate	Eager	Jaded	Rejected
Afraid	Ecstatic	Jealous	Relieved
Agitated	Embarrassed	Jolly	Remorseful
Aggressive	Emotional	Jittery	Revulsed
Amused	Enraged	Jubilant	Sad
Angry	Enthusiastic	Kind	Satisfied
Anxious	Exasperated	Keen	Scared
Annoyed	Exuberant	Laid back	Shamed
Astonished	Fascinated	Lonely	Smug
Bored	Fearful	Mad	Sorry
Blue	Flustered	Merry	Stingy
Bitter	Frightened	Modest	Sympathetic
Calm	Furious	Mortified	Tender
Caring	Generous	Naughty	Threatened
Cheerful	Gloomy	Nervous	Timid
Composed	Glum	Open	Tranquil
Crabby	Grouchy	Optimistic	Trusting
Crazed	Guilty	Outgoing	Uncomfortable
Cross	Happy	Panicked	Upset
Defeated	Homesick	Passionate	Vain
Delighted	Horrified	Pensive	Vengeful
Depressed	Hurt	Pessimistic	Vivacious
Disgusted	Infatuated	Proud	Wary
Dismayed	Insulted	Quiet	Weary
Distracted	Irritated	Quirky	Worried
	Insecure		Zealous

Resources and Citations

The American Academy of Suicidology
https://www.suicidology.org/resources

Bannink, Fredrike. 2010. 1001 Solution-Focused
Questions: Handbook for Solution-Focused
Interviewing. W.W. Norton and Company.

Bowlby, John. 1969. Attachment and loss. Basic Books

Brown, Brené. 2010. The Gifts of Imperfection. Let Go
of Who You Think You're Supposed to be and
Embrace Who You Are. Hazelden Publishing.

Centers for Disease Control and Prevention
https://www.cdc.gov/

Dinkmeyer, Don; McKay, Gary; Dinkmeyer Jr. Don
2008, The Parent's Handbook: Systematic Training for
Effective Parenting. STEP Publishers.

Diaz, Karen. 2018. Within: Making Peace with Food
and Body Image to Create a Healthy Family and Home.
Lioncrest Publishing.

Eldridge, Sherry. 1999. Twenty Things Adopted Kids
Wish Their Adoptive Parents Knew. Delta.

Forbes, Heather and Post, B. Brian. 2006. Beyond
Consequences Logic, and Control: A Love-Based
Approach to Helping Attachment-Challenged Children
With Severe Behaviors.

Hardyment, Christina. 1983, 2007. <u>Dream Babies: Childcare Advice From John Locke to Gina Ford</u>. Harper Collins.

Harlow H. F., Dodsworth R. O., & Harlow M. K. (1965). Total social isolation in monkeys. *Proceedings of the National Academy of Sciences of the United States of America.*

Jaffe, Janet; Diamond, David; Diamond, Martha. 2005. <u>Unsung Lullabies: Understanding and Coping with Infertility.</u> Griffin.

Johnson, Cynthia, Butter, Eric and Scahill, Lawrence, Eds. 2018. <u>Parent Training for Autism Spectrum Disorder: Improving the Quality of Life for Children and Their Families</u> 1st Edition. American Psychological Association.

Massimo, Matthew and Price, Sofia. 2015. <u>Stepparenting: Becoming A Stepparent: A Blended Family Guide to: Parenting, Raising Children, Family Relationships and Step Families.</u> Amazon Books.

McBride, Karyl. 2009. <u>Will I Ever Be Good Enough?: Healing the Daughters of Narcissistic Mothers.</u> Atria Books.

National Center for Education Statistics. <u>https://nces.ed.gov/</u>

NYU Study Examines Top High School Students' Stress and Coping Mechanisms. 2015. News Release.

O'Connor, Rosemary. 2015. <u>A Sober Mom's Guide to Recovery: Taking Care of Yourself to Take Care of Your Kids.</u> Hazelden Publishing.

Patterson, Kerry; Grenny, Joseph; McMillan, Ron; Switzler, Al. 2002. <u>Crucial Conversations: Tools for Talking When Stakes are High.</u> McGraw Hill.

Pavlov, I. P. (1927). Conditioned reflexes: an investigation of the physiological activity of the cerebral cortex. Oxford, England: Oxford Univ. Press.

Piaget, Jean and Inhelder, Barbel. 1969. <u>The Psychology of the Child</u>. Basic Books.

Ryan, Gail; Leversee, Tom; Lane, Sandy; 2013. <u>Juvenile Sexual Offending</u>, 3rd Ed. Wiley.

Serani, Deborah. 2013. <u>Depression and Your Child: A Guide for Parents and Caregivers</u>. Rowman & Littlefield.

Sears, William and Sears, Martha. 1993. <u>The Baby Book : Everything You Need to Know about Your Baby from Birth to Age Two.</u> Little, Brown and Company.

Sparks, Sarah. 2016, August 11. <u>Student Mobility: How it Affects Learning</u>. Education Week.

Spock, Benjamin. 2011. <u>Dr. Spock's Baby and Child Care: 9th Edition.</u> Pocket Books.

Acknowledgements

I want to thank my book club ladies, first of all, for listening to my idea and being so encouraging! Shout out to Joan, Rose, Krista, Lisa, and Danielle who consistently show up for me and each other over the past almost two years. Thank you, Jen Sincero, whose books got me to stop blocking myself and start believing in my worth. I never thought I would be saying that about an author and not a therapist. My amazing volunteer editors, Danielle, Sarah, Susan and Zoe, who generously picked over the manuscript to bring it up to standard. My sister, Liz, for our lifetime relationship that keeps evolving, and brother Hugh for teaching me that family is about love not blood. To my pup, Rocky, who kept my feet warm while I was writing, sometimes a little too warm. And at last, to my mom, Emily, who was not a perfect parent, but loved her children perfectly.

Photo credits:

Alice Riley, self-portrait.

Cover design: Alice Riley

The High Risk Cycle can be downloaded as a printable PDF here: www.aliceriley.net/bonus-materials

51251443R00109

Made in the USA
Lexington, KY
01 September 2019